THE ATLAS OF
UNUSUAL
LANGUAGES

Published by Collins
An imprint of HarperCollins Publishers
Westerhill Road
Bishopbriggs
Glasgow G64 2QT

HarperCollins Publishers
1st Floor, Watermarque Building, Ringsend Road, Dublin 4, Ireland

collins.reference@harpercollins.co.uk
collins.co.uk

First published 2021
© HarperCollins Publishers 2021
Text © Zoran Nikolić 2021

Photographs and text credits © see Acknowledgements on page 238–9
Maps © Collins Bartholomew Ltd 2021

A catalogue record for this book is available from the British Library

ISBN 978-0-00-846959-7

10 9 8 7 6 5 4 3 2 1

Printed in Bosnia and Herzegovina by GPS Group

All mapping in this atlas is generated from Collins Bartholomew digital databases.
Collins Bartholomew, the UK's leading independent geographical information supplier,
can provide a digital, custom, and premium mapping service to a variety of markets.
e-mail: collinsbartholomew@harpercollins.co.uk
or visit our website at: collinsbartholomew.com

THE ATLAS OF
UNUSUAL
LANGUAGES

ZORAN NIKOLIĆ

(Taa)

CONTENTS

INTRODUCTION

by Ivana Perišić, professor of Serbian language and literature

Language is essential to our way of life. The need to convey our thoughts and feelings to each other, and to share information, has existed throughout the history of humankind. We do not know at what point people first started using the spoken word, but what began as gestures and simple sounds has evolved over time into a multitude of highly developed languages.

Throughout human history, people have moved from one area to another, perhaps searching for fertile land or in response to other factors such as conflict, climate change or religion. This migration has led to the creation of nations, the redrawing of borders and the mixing of people – and therefore of the languages they speak. As a result, it is rare for a language to remain 'pure', staying in its original form without the influence of other tongues. The constant need for people to understand one another and express themselves has meant that languages have changed over time, which in turn has led to the creation of new languages and the extinction of others. Today, languages are disappearing much more quickly than new ones are being created.

There are an estimated 7,000 languages in use across the world today. Of these, English is the most widely spoken. The number of speakers a language has is the main factor affecting its survival. Those languages with a high number of speakers, such as Russian, Chinese and Hindi, tend to remain intact within their homelands. However, with the development of technology, they too are being affected by external influences. For a language to survive, it must adapt while at the same time keeping its individual features and serving a purpose. Even some languages regarded as 'dead', such as Latin, ancient Greek, ancient Slavic and Coptic, live on in some way, because we use them in literature, science, law and religion.

The status of a language within a particular country can change with each generation. Some countries have more than one official language. The Republic of Ireland, for instance, has Irish as its first official language and English as its second, but it is only Irish that is written into the constitution as the 'national' language, even though it now has fewer speakers. In Germany, languages such as Turkish, Serbian and Greek, which have been brought into the country by immigrants, may not have the same official status as the German language, but they are being increasingly included on official government websites. While members of a minority population of a country may use both their mother tongue and the language of the country in which they live, the very concept of a 'mother tongue' becomes less meaningful when children are raised bilingual or even trilingual without one of the languages being clearly dominant.

This book illustrates the fascinating and complex relationship between people, language and geography. How is it that in some areas, a language is spoken that is almost completely incomprehensible to other inhabitants of the same country? Why do some languages change, and what determines how long these changes last? You will find the answers within these pages. You will also discover new facts, some of which may challenge your understanding of the connection between language and place.

The author has set out to enhance your knowledge of languages in a clear and interesting way. And so, dear reader, sit back, absorb and enjoy this selection of unusual languages.

WHAT ARE LANGUAGE ISLANDS?

We all know what an **island** is: a body of land, smaller than a continent, that is surrounded by water on all sides. This water can be a river, a lake, a sea or an ocean. This definition is quite clear and unambiguous.

But what is a **language island**? Following the logic of the island definition, we could say that *a language island is a territory where a particular language is spoken, and which is surrounded by one or more significantly larger languages.* This is a conditional definition, which will, more or less, be used throughout this book.

At this point it is essential to understand the difference between **language** and **dialect**. These terms can be more difficult to define, since some linguists may view two dialects as two separate languages, while a large number of their colleagues might argue that they are two completely independent, albeit close, languages. Politics can complicate matters too, whereby one country may 'appropriate' the language of a neighbouring country, with the aim of increasing its size and prestige. However, this is usually of little interest to the linguist, so for the purposes of this book, the following simple scenario can be used to differentiate between language and dialect:

- We have person A and person B.
- Person A knows only language A and has never been in contact with speakers of language B.
- Person B knows only language B and has never been in contact with speakers of language A.
- If person A and person B each speak their own language and understand each other well, then languages A and B are actually dialects.
- If person A and person B need a translator in order to understand each other, then they are speaking two separate languages, even though these may be close.

The aim of this book is to present a selection of current language islands from around the world, as well as some interesting historical ones that have been absorbed into one of the larger languages over time.

Please note that the author of this book, introduced on page 240, is not a linguist and the book is not intended to be read as a scientific work. Instead, it's simply a collection of some interesting linguistic curiosities and should be viewed as such.

LANGUAGE ISOLATES

WHAT ARE LANGUAGE ISOLATES?

In order to appreciate the linguistic diversity of our planet, we must begin with the fact that there are currently about 7,000 living languages in use around the world. In addition, several hundred extinct languages are being studied, with efforts being made to revive some of these and return them to everyday use. Most languages are grouped into **language families**. The concept of language families is based on the assumption that dialects of languages often evolve into separate but related languages over time. This can be described in terms of a **language tree**, where the proto-language forms the main 'trunk', and this becomes divided into language 'branches', representing the languages that have relatively recently separated from the proto-language. The 'crown' becomes more and more dense over time as new dialects develop from the branches. Although some branches will fall off over time, as languages become extinct, other branches may develop into a new language family of their own.

We can see an example of a language tree in the illustration on the opposite page. The trunk represents the *Germanic language*, which itself formed from a branch of the Indo-European language family. The trunk eventually divided into its descendants of *West*, *North* and *East Germanic* branches, and thus the Germanic language became a separate language family.

Over time, North Germanic further divided into new branches, becoming a new family; today those branches are Swedish, Danish, Norwegian, Icelandic, etc. Unfortunately, the East Germanic branch is truncated, since all languages of that family simply died out. In the distant future, some surviving languages could be divided into new branches, or they could disappear altogether.

The exceptions to this rule are the **language isolates**. These are *languages for which it is not possible to establish a connection with either the rest of the language branch or the complete family*. Examples of such languages are Armenian, Albanian and Greek, which have been unequivocally identified as part of the Indo-European language family, but according to current knowledge, the three languages are separate branches, with no connection to other branches of the Indo-European family.

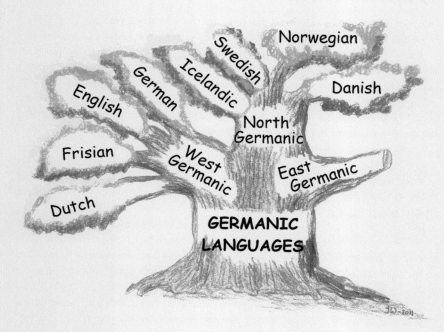

There are also language isolates for which no connection can be established with any language family. These include the Basque language, which is used today within part of the Basque Country in Spain and France, the language of the Ainu people in Japan, the Burushaski language in northern Pakistan, and the ancient Sumerian language. Despite the great efforts of many scholars, no undisputed connection of these languages to any other living language has been found so far. (Assumptions and unproven hypotheses about connections with some extinct languages do exist, for example some linguists believe that the extinct Aquitaine language was either an ancestor or a relative of the Basque language.)

EUROPE

Although a large number of languages are spoken in Europe and they have differing numbers of speakers, most of these languages belong to a huge family of **Indo-European** languages (which has a total of 3.2 billion speakers worldwide). In fact, when looking at the map of language families, Europe looks like a monotonous Indo-European sea with only a few islands of other families, of which the most important is the **Uralic** language family, also known as the **Finno-Ugric** group (with 25 million speakers in total). Today, the languages from that group are mostly spoken in Central Europe (Hungary) and Northern Europe (Finland, Estonia and parts of Russia). Some languages of the disputed **Altaic** family (a proposed language family rejected by many comparative linguists) – primarily Turkish and Azerbaijani – are spoken in several locations in the southeast of the continent. Worldwide, there are hundreds of millions of speakers of languages from this family, depending on which languages are considered to be members. The languages of one of the smallest language families, the **Kartvelian** (a total of 5 million speakers), are also spoken in this region; the Georgian language makes up three-quarters of the speakers in this family. However, one language in Europe stands out from all other languages and all language families. It is the small Basque language. With fewer than a million speakers, it does not show a connection with any existing language in Europe or the world, which makes it a typical language isolate.

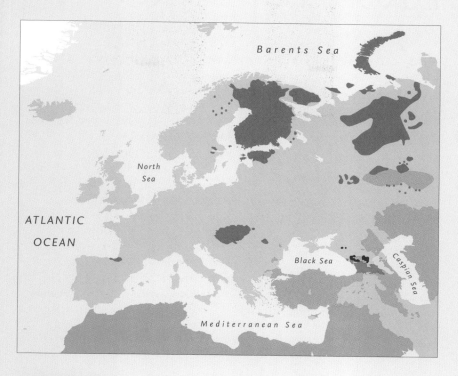

Barents Sea

North Sea

ATLANTIC OCEAN

Black Sea

Caspian Sea

Mediterranean Sea

LANGUAGES

AFRO-ASIATIC   ALTAIC   BASQUE   CASPIAN

INDO-EUROPEAN   KARTVELIAN   PONTIC   URALIC

BASQUE, FRANCE/SPAIN

In the far west of Europe, where the gigantic mountain range of the Pyrenees descends towards the Bay of Biscay and the Atlantic Ocean, lies the land of the **Basques**, whose language is (probably) the oldest living European language. There is no common opinion among experts as to where the Basques came from: it is widely assumed that their ancestors came from North Africa more than 15,000 years ago; though according to some sources, the Basques may have originated in the Caucasus. The only fact that has been established with certainty is that this language is completely isolated from all known living and extinct languages, and it is the only surviving **Paleo-European** language.

The Spanish–French border divides the historic region of **Basque Country** (**Euskal Herria** in Basque) into two areas, of which 86 per cent of the area belongs to Spain (Southern Basque Country; Hegoalde in Basque) and the remaining 14 per cent to France (Northern Basque Country; Iparralde in Basque).

The Southern Basque Country consists of two autonomous communities: Basque Autonomous Community (Euskadi in Basque), where **Basque** is the official language alongside **Spanish**, and the Autonomous Community of Navarre (Nafarroa in Basque), where only parts have Basque as their official language. Across Navarre as a whole, only about 15 per cent of the total population uses the Basque language every day.

The entire historical region of the Basque Country has just under 3 million inhabitants, of whom about 700,000 people speak the Basque language (approximately 25 per cent of the population of the seven historical provinces that make up this region).

However, a large number of students enrol in schools that teach in the standard Basque language and they increasingly use it in everyday situations, as well as in the media, social networks and official documents.

Traditional Basque carnival in northern Navarre, Spain

AFRICA

The continent of Africa is home to one of the oldest recorded languages, the ancient Egyptian language, whose first texts were written about 5,000 years ago. Today, the Coptic language, the successor of that ancient language, is still used in the Coptic Church, as well as in everyday speech among the very small number of remaining Copts. All languages spoken in Africa can be divided into several very large language families: **Afroasiatic**, **Nilo-Saharan**, **Niger-Congo**, **Bantu**, **Khoisan** (geographical grouping of languages, not linguistic), **Indo-European** and **Austronesian** in Madagascar. The total number of indigenous languages is about 2,000, and in Nigeria alone there are almost 500. A large number of these languages are unclassified, primarily due to lack of information, and some are considered language isolates.

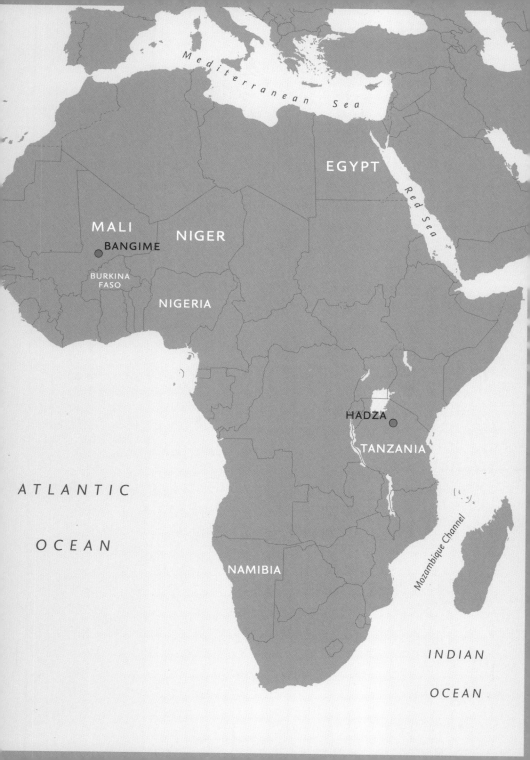

HADZA, TANZANIA

The **Hadza** or **Hadzabe** people (meaning 'people') have inhabited the area around **Lake Eyasi** in Tanzania, south of the Serengeti National Park and Ngorongoro Crater, for tens of thousands of years. Archeological findings show that this area has been inhabited by hunter-gatherers, such as the Hadza, for at least 50,000 years, while the **Bantu** people came to this region much later, about 2,000 years ago. There is a (not widely accepted) theory that the entire human race consists of three 'branches': the Hadza people, the **Jul'hoan** people of Namibia, and all other people. This idea is based on the fact that the Hadza and Jul'hoan use clicks in their speech, as well as having the most divergent known mitochondrial DNA of any human population, indicating that they are descended from those that first separated from the rest of the human 'tree'.

The Hadza tribe currently has about 1,300 members, of whom approximately 1,000 use their ancient isolated **Hadza** language. Most children still learn this language, so it is not considered to be in danger of extinction. If one wants to learn to count in a foreign language, Hadza could be a great choice for quick learning: number one is *itchâme*, number two is *piye*, while *ace* means a lot. And that's it. For all other numbers, borrowings from neighbouring languages are used, primarily from **Swahili**.

The Hadza people are distinct for being an egalitarian society, where all members of the tribe have a similar social status, regardless of age or gender. Also, it is common for a large number of people to help mothers with raising children, whether they are related or not (although, given the size and age of the tribe, it can be assumed that some family ties exist between all of its members). When tribe members die, their bodies are left in the bush for the hyenas to do their part. The Hadza do not use a calendar, do not grow any vegetables or cereals, and get food from animals exclusively by hunting. They always try to live in harmony with the nature that surrounds them.

Hadzabe hunter

BANGIME, MALI

The land of the **Dogons** is a large region in the states of Mali, Burkina Faso and Niger, inhabited by the Dogons, an ethnic group known for its colourful, often unusually large masks, striking wooden sculptures and distinctive architecture. For a long time, the Dogons suffered strong pressure to accept Islam, so in the period from the fourteenth to the sixteenth centuries, they began to move their villages from the plains to **Bandiagara Escarpment**, a limestone massif about 500 metres high and 150 kilometres long. There, on hard-to-reach plateaus and gorges, they found relative safety.

Today, there are almost one million Dogon people and they speak a large number of mostly related languages (about twenty languages and at least as many dialects), which are jointly considered to be a separate branch of the Niger-Congo language family. However, one group of about 3,500 Dogons speaks a **Bangime** language that has nothing to do with the other Dogon languages. In fact, this language seems to have nothing to do with any language in Africa or the world.

The **Bangande** tribe, as they call themselves, lives in rather hidden canyons in the depths of the Bandiagara Escarpment; the main settlement is **Bounou**, but there are six other smaller villages around it. It is possible that their language is actually a remnant of the language of the natives of this massif, which was spoken long before the arrival of the Dogons. What is unusual is that the Bangande consider themselves Dogons, and their language to be one of the Dogon languages or dialects, while other Dogons consider the Bangande to belong to neither their ethnic nor linguistic family. According to Bangande stories, during the slave trade, some enslaved people escaped their enslavers in the vicinity of these villages. The Bangande tribe would then accept the enslaved people into their village as free men, and many remained in the village, where they would learn the language and become assimilated.

The village of Bounou is the main settlement of the Bangande people

ASIA

The Asian continent is a giant among all other continents in terms of size and population, but also in terms of the number of languages. Roughly speaking, the largest language families include **Sino-Tibetan**, **Indo-European**, **Turkic**, **Austronesian**, **Japanese**, **Korean** and a few more. However, Asia is also home to a number of language isolates, that is, languages for which it is not possible to prove any connection with other languages. Until recently, both Japanese and Korean were classed as language isolates. However, recent research concludes that Korean is actually a Koreanic language family, consisting of the Korean language itself as well as the language of Jeju Island and possibly the Yukjin language, which is spoken in the extreme northeast of North Korea (though this may be a dialect). The situation is similar with the Japanese language, which was previously considered a language isolate, but today is regarded as a Japonic language family, consisting of Japanese, the Ryukyuan languages, and the small language of Hachijō, which is spoken on two islands south of Tokyo.

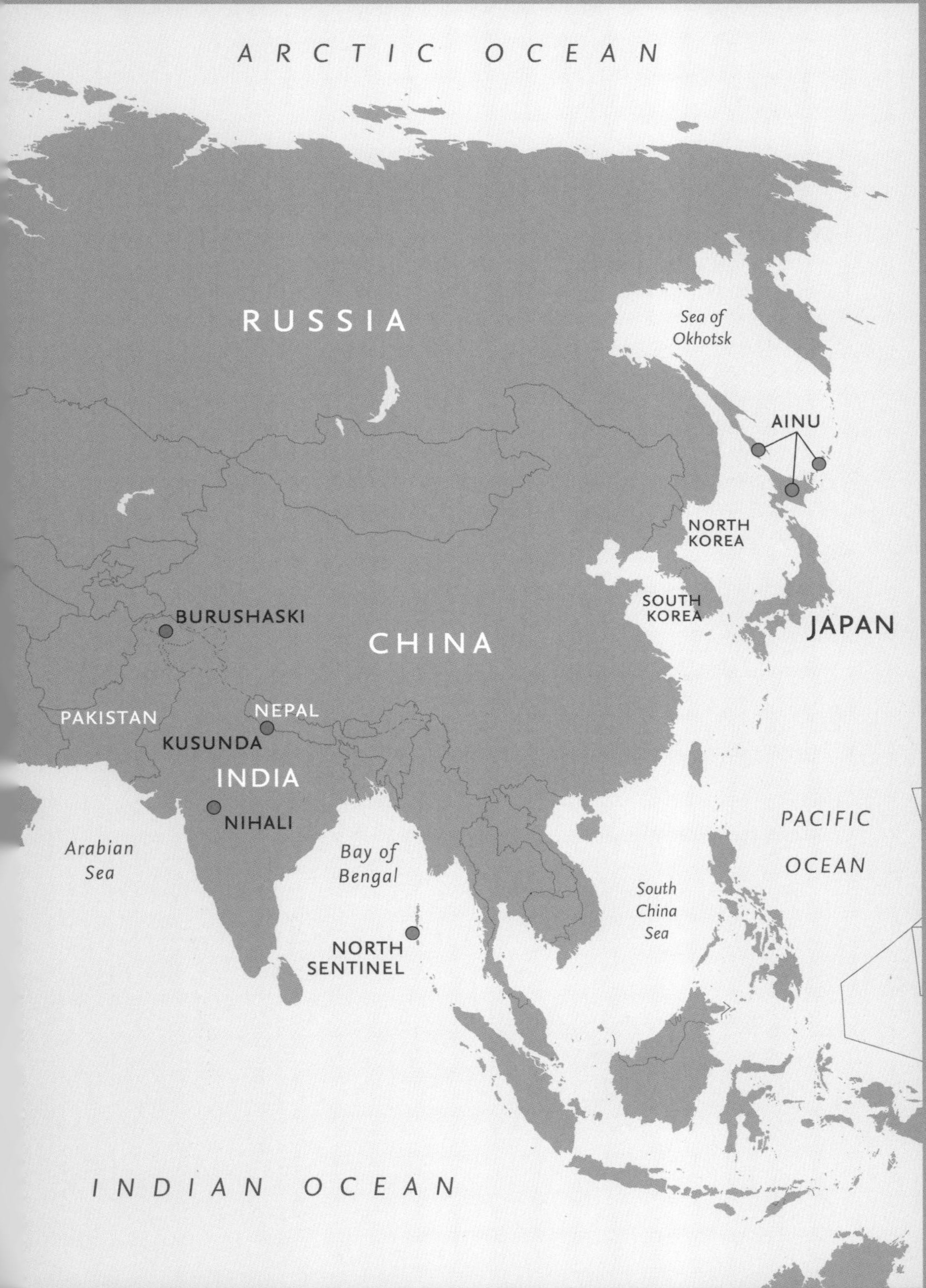

ARCTIC OCEAN

RUSSIA

Sea of
Okhotsk

AINU

NORTH
KOREA

SOUTH
KOREA

JAPAN

BURUSHASKI

CHINA

PAKISTAN

NEPAL

KUSUNDA

INDIA

NIHALI

Arabian
Sea

Bay of
Bengal

South
China
Sea

PACIFIC
OCEAN

NORTH
SENTINEL

INDIAN OCEAN

AINU, JAPAN

Ainu is the ancient language of the northern Japanese island of **Hokkaido**, the Russian island of **Sakhalin** and the **Kuril Islands**. It is believed that the earliest ancestors of today's **Ainu** people crossed to the Japanese archipelago more than 15,000 years ago. These first settlers formed the **Jomon** culture, which lasted until about 300 BC, when the **Yayoi** people began migrating from the Korean Peninsula. With the extensive mixing of the Yayoi and Jomon, the Japanese nation was born, under the considerable dominance of the Yayoi. According to one theory, a group of Jomon people decided to escape this situation by fleeing to the north, where they formed the Ainu people, while another group fled to the south and inhabited the Ryukyu Islands.

The most difficult period for the Ainu began in the second half of the nineteenth century, when the newly formed single Japanese nation placed a total ban on the use of Ainu language, as well as their customs and way of life. The total collapse of the Ainu people and language led to almost complete assimilation, which is probably what would have happened had one Ainu, Shigeru Kayano, not finally been elected a member of the Japanese parliament at the end of the twentieth century. He fought fiercely in the parliament for the rights of his people, and in 2019, 13 years after his death, a bill was passed which officially recognized the Ainu as an indigenous people of Japan. Unfortunately, only a few dozen of them use their language every day. The village of **Nibutani** (**Niptani** in Ainu), with 80 per cent Ainu, is probably the most ethnically homogeneous Ainu settlement in Japan today. This was where Shigeru Kayano was born.

The latest genetic research shows that the Ainu are related to the indigenous peoples of the Alaskan and Canadian Pacific coasts, such as the **Tlingit** people. Further research has established that the ancestors of the Ainu and those indigenous peoples may have originated from an area not far from the almost-quadripoint of Russia, Kazakhstan, China and Mongolia.

The Ainu's compatriots on Sakhalin have been almost completely assimilated, to the point that, according to the latest data, there are only about a hundred Ainu in Russia.

The Kuril Islands were also inhabited by the Ainu, including the southern part of that archipelago, over which Russia and Japan have been arguing since the end of the Second World War.

Traditional Ainu dance at the Ainu Museum, Shiraoi, Hokkaido

KUSUNDA, NEPAL

Somewhere in a lush green rainforest in central Nepal lives a small tribe that doesn't have a word for green in its vocabulary! According to some linguists, because greenery is all around them, there is no need to describe the obvious.

This little tribe is known as **Kusunda**, or **Ban Raja** (*ban* = forest, *raja* = king), though they call themselves **Mihaq**. Until recently, they were hunter-gatherers, who would occasionally exchange their captured prey with neighbours through the so-called *silent trade*, which is a way of trading between two groups of people who do not speak each other's language. The Kusunda would leave their captured prey out for the Nepalese farmers, who would then come and leave their agricultural produce in exchange. If they were satisfied with the offered goods, the Kusunda would take it, and the farmers would also take the captured animal.

Today, only a few elderly people are fluent in this ancient language, so it is considered critically endangered and on the verge of extinction.

The Kusunda were historically considered to be wild people from the forest, so many members would conceal their ethnic origin. And the origin of the tribe itself could be another remarkable feature of this people: there are researchers who claim that Kusunda are direct descendants of the first humans, who set out from Africa towards Australia, following the southern coasts of Asia. Alternatively, some linguists believe that the languages **Kusunda**, **Burushaski**, **Nihali** and **Vedda** are among the last remnants of archaic languages spoken on the Indian subcontinent before the immigration of Indo-European and Sino-Tibetan peoples (although they do not belong to the **Dravidian** languages, who are also native to the Indian subcontinent).

Gyani Maiya Sen, thought to be the last fluent speaker of the Kusunda language, died in 2020

BURUSHASKI, PAKISTAN/INDIA

At the point where the mighty mountain ranges of the Himalaya, Hindu Kush and Karakoram meet, at an altitude of about 2,500 metres, where the water is pure and the air is fresh, there lies the **Hunza Valley**, home of **Burushaski**, another language isolate. This valley is inhabited by the **Burusho** people, also known as the **Hunza**. According to legend (and claims on social media), these people are blessed with extremely long lives and the absence of most modern diseases. In addition, there are numerous theories that the Hunza originated from several soldiers of the invincible army of Alexander the Great. This 'magical' valley is located right on the eastern borders of the ruler's ancient **Macedonian Empire**, in the area of Gilgit-Baltistan (a Pakistani-administered area of the disputed Kashmir region).

Science has a different opinion to the legends and social media. And science says the Hunza do not live longer than the average person in northern Pakistan and the surrounding regions. They may be less likely to suffer from diseases that plague people in more urban and polluted environments, but they also have a large number of diseases of their own. Genetic analysis of a random selection of the inhabitants of the Hunza Valley shows that they have absolutely no genes that are characteristic of the Greeks.

As for the language, the Burusho really do speak a language that has no confirmed connection with any living language, or even with the languages of the peoples and tribes that surround them. Although various connections have been suggested between Burushaski and other languages – such as **North Caucasus**, Kartvelian (the most well-known representative of which is **Georgian**), and the **Yenisei** (of which only the **Ket** language survives today, spoken by about 200 people in central Siberia), and even the Basque language thousands of kilometres away – none of these theories is widely accepted.

Hunza women with their characteristic hats

Today, fewer than 100,000 people in the northern Pakistani Hunza, **Nagar**, **Yasin** and **Ishkoman** valleys speak Burushaski, as well as about 350 people around Hari Parbat hill in **Srinagar**, the summer capital of the Indian Union Territory of Jammu and Kashmir. These Indian speakers of Burushaski are descendants of a small group that was expelled from what is now Pakistan almost 150 years ago so their language is somewhat different from the Pakistani variants, but the mutual intelligibility is still high.

NIHALI AND NORTH SENTINEL LANGUAGES, INDIA

One of the language isolates in India is **Nihali** (**kalṭo manḍi** in Nihali). The speakers of this unusual language – no more than 2,000 of them – live in the southernmost part of the Indian state of **Madhya Pradesh**, on the border with the state of Maharashtra. What is unusual about this language is the fact that as much as 75 per cent of its vocabulary is borrowed from neighbouring languages.

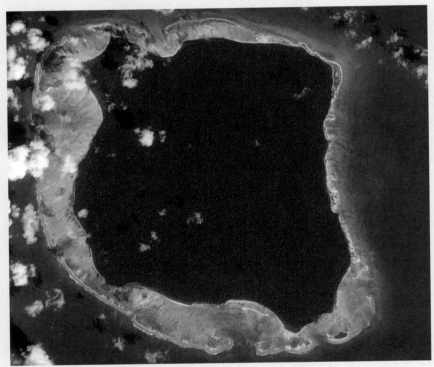

North Sentinel Island

And the remaining 25 per cent of Nihali words have been confusing linguists for a long time, as they have been unable to determine the origin of this language, or its connection with other languages.

One theory is that Nihali is a remnant of an ancient language, which over time has absorbed numerous words from neighbouring Indo-European languages. Another is that it is not a 'real' language at all, but a jargon or secret language, invented by the locals so that they can converse in front of others without fear of being understood.

Southeast of mainland India, in the Bay of Bengal, is the Indian Union Territory of the Andaman and Nicobar Islands. This archipelago is home to many languages, both large (**Bengali**, **Hindi**, **Tamil**, **Telugu**...) and small. One of the small, little-known languages is that of the inhabitants of **North Sentinel**.

Here are some facts that are known about the **Sentinelese** (also known as the **Sentineli**) and their language: about 50 to 500 people live on the island of North Sentinel. They are thought to be the direct descendants of the first group of people to leave Africa – about 60,000 years ago – and head to Australia. Their language is regarded as unclassified or belonging to language isolates. The difficulty in studying this language is that the Sentinelese are very private and have little contact with the outside world. One attempt revealed that the Sentinelese couldn't understand the other inhabitants of the archipelago, suggesting their language is not related to any of the languages of the surrounding islands. For now, the conclusion is simple: we don't know what the Sentinelese call themselves; we do not know what they call their language; we have no idea what they call their island.

At the end of the twentieth century, India decided to impose a ban on access to the island of North Sentinel, partly to avoid conflict between Sentinelese and visitors, but also to prevent the transmission of potentially deadly diseases to this isolated group of people. Today, the island of North Sentinel functions as a kind of miniature independent state under Indian protection.

NEW GUINEA

With an area of over 800,000 square kilometres – about the size of Turkey – the island of New Guinea is the second largest island in the world and the largest island in the southern hemisphere (Australia, which is a larger landmass, is classed as a continent). Politically, it is divided into two almost equal parts, which are split between the continents of Asia and Oceania. The independent state of Papua New Guinea (PNG) covers 462,840 square kilometres, has 9 million inhabitants and is located on the eastern part of the island, while the western part belongs to Indonesia and contains the provinces of Papua and West Papua. This part measures 420,540 square kilometres and has 4.5 million inhabitants.

An interesting feature of the island of New Guinea is the vast number of languages spoken on it: it is believed that between 250 and 300 languages are used in Indonesian Papua, while over 1,000 languages are spoken in PNG! These dizzying numbers are the result of a number of factors: the island of New Guinea is intersected by high, almost impassable, mountains; between these mountains there are also difficult-to-cross swamps and fast-flowing mountain rivers; the first people settled in New Guinea more than 40,000 years ago, and in all this time they have rarely left their valleys, surrounded as they are by those mountains, swamps and rivers. All of these factors have influenced the independent development of hundreds of languages, which today are grouped together as the **Papuan** languages. This grouping is purely on the grounds of geographical proximity, since there is no closeness or similarity between most of the languages themselves. Papuan languages are exclusively spoken on New Guinea; they do not belong to the **Austronesian** family, nor to the indigenous Australian languages. Among these hundreds of Papuan languages, there are several dozen language isolates.

South China Sea

PACIFIC OCEAN

INDONESIA

ABINOMN

TAYAP

KUOT

PAPUA NEW GUINEA

Arafura Sea

NDIAN CEAN

Coral Sea

AUSTRALIA

Tasman Sea

ABINOMN, INDONESIA

Deep in the forests of the northern part of Indonesian Papua, next to the Taritatu river, there is a village whose roughly 300 inhabitants speak the **Abinomn** language (also known as **Avinomen** or **Foya**). Little is known about this language isolate, and the sad fact is that most younger people are slowly switching to the **Mander** language of the neighbouring tribe, which is also critically endangered and on the verge of extinction. It is assumed that there are no more than fifty true speakers of the Abinomn language today.

TAYAP, PAPUA NEW GUINEA

At 1,126 kilometres long, the Sepik river is the longest river in New Guinea. It flows through the northern part of PNG for almost its entire course, with just a short stretch passing into Indonesia. Not far from where the Sepik flows into the Bismarck Sea, is the village of **Gapun** with about 150 inhabitants, of whom less than fifty speak the language isolate of **Tayap**. Today, most Gapun residents consider the language obsolete, and young people are increasingly switching to **Tok Pisin**, one of the three official languages of PNG. An interesting custom is associated with this village and its inhabitants: after giving birth, a woman usually goes to a special, secluded hut where she stays until the baby smiles for the first time. This custom allows mothers to have a short 'time out', because they will decide when the baby's first smile is seen.

KUOT, PAPUA NEW GUINEA

About 35,000 years ago, the first human settlers arrived on **New Ireland**, a large, elongated island northeast of New Guinea. The fact that New Ireland was never connected by land to any larger mainland, even at a time when the sea level was at its lowest, proves that these people were already competent seafarers. Around 1,000 BC, a large group of Austronesian peoples sailed to this island, gradually becoming the majority population. Today, New Ireland is home to about 120,000 people, speaking approximately twenty languages; of that number, only one language – **Kuot** – belongs to the Papuan (i.e. non-Austronesian) languages.

The **Kuot** people number just under 2,500, but their language is spoken by fewer than 1,500. It is believed that the Kuots are the descendants of those first settlers who arrived on New Ireland 35 millennia ago. Although they have managed to maintain their language for this long – it is spoken in a dozen small villages in the central part of the island – today it is under enormous threat from Tok Pisin, to which the youth are increasingly switching. It is sad that, along with the language, various customs characteristic of the Kuots are slowly disappearing, such as the casting of spells and similar magical rituals, which have long been carried out in this ancient language.

Traditional 'malagan' dances are now rare among the Kuot people

AUSTRALIA

Although sparsely populated, Australia is home to about 300 indigenous languages, a large number of which are language isolates, with the rest being divided into nearly thirty language families. Within the families, the connections between the individual languages are not always clear, nor are they clear between the families themselves. There are also a number of languages that are described as unclassified, which means that not enough data has yet been collected to determine whether they belong to a language family or are, in fact, language isolates. Unfortunately, many languages will remain unclassified or, even if they are classified in a family, will be poorly known, since almost all of the indigenous languages are endangered or on the verge of extinction. It is believed that only a little over one hundred languages are actually in use, that almost 90 per cent are critically endangered, and that speakers are passing their mother tongue on to their children in fewer than fifteen of the languages. The largest number of language isolates is located in Top End, the northern part of Northern Territory.

South
China
Sea

PACIFIC

OCEAN

INDONESIA

PAPUA
NEW
GUINEA

Arafura Sea

TIWI

LARAGIYA

WAGIMAN

NDIAN

OCEAN

Coral
Sea

AUSTRALIA

Tasman

Sea

LARAGIYA

Of the once extensive **Larrakia** people, only a few people remain who have some knowledge of this little-known language. The language of **Larrakia** (also known as **Laragiya** and formerly known locally as **Gulumirrgin**) is not fully known at this time, and it is not certain whether it is a language isolate or part of a local (also little-known) small language family. Its few speakers have only limited knowledge of certain words and expressions. The Larrakia Nation (self-designation: 'Saltwater People') is still relatively large, and its 2,000 members are especially proud of the fact that Darwin, the capital of Northern Territory, was built on their land.

WAGIMAN

Near the town of Pine Creek in Northern Territory, primarily in the small village of **Kybrook Farm**, live the few dozen members of the **Wagiman** people, several of whom are elderly people who speak the language isolate of the same name. This language is characterized by extremely complicated grammar, which is one of the reasons why young people are increasingly switching to **Australian Kriol** and English, as languages that give them a better chance of finding their desired (or any) job. According to linguists, this language will become extinct in a couple of decades, if not sooner. The Wagiman people own Tjuwaliyn (Douglas) Hot Springs Nature Park, known for both its hot springs and locally significant sacred sites. Here, Wagiman women perform religious and cultural rituals; locations considered to be sacred are forbidden for men to visit.

TIWI

The language isolate of **Tiwi** is spoken by more than 2,000 members of the **Tiwi** people (or **Tunuvivi**) in the **Tiwi Islands** (**Ratuati Irara** in Tiwi: 'two islands'), off the coast of Northern Territory. This is one of only a few indigenous languages that is being successfully passed on from parents to children. However, this language is also going through an unusual change: younger people mostly speak a significantly simplified version of the language, known as **Modern Tiwi**, which has been considerably influenced by the English language. This version is now used by practically all people under the age of 30, as well as many older people, leaving **Traditional Tiwi** possibly being used by fewer than fifty (elderly) people. Many speakers of the modern version have difficulty understanding the traditional version. In the Tiwi Islands, the local language is taught in all schools as a first language.

Tiwi burial 'Pukamani' poles

NORTH AMERICA

Before European colonization, hundreds or even thousands of languages were spoken throughout the Americas. These languages were grouped into dozens of different families, of which today the largest are: **Uto-Aztecan**, consisting of about sixty languages and just under 2 million speakers; **Na-Dene**, with a total of about 200,000 speakers (the most well-known languages of this family are the languages of the Apache and Navajo); and the **Algic/Algonquian**, with about 100,000 speakers. In addition to these language families, a large number of language isolates exist (though their numbers are decreasing), for which no connection has been established with any other indigenous languages. We will get to know some of these languages in this section.

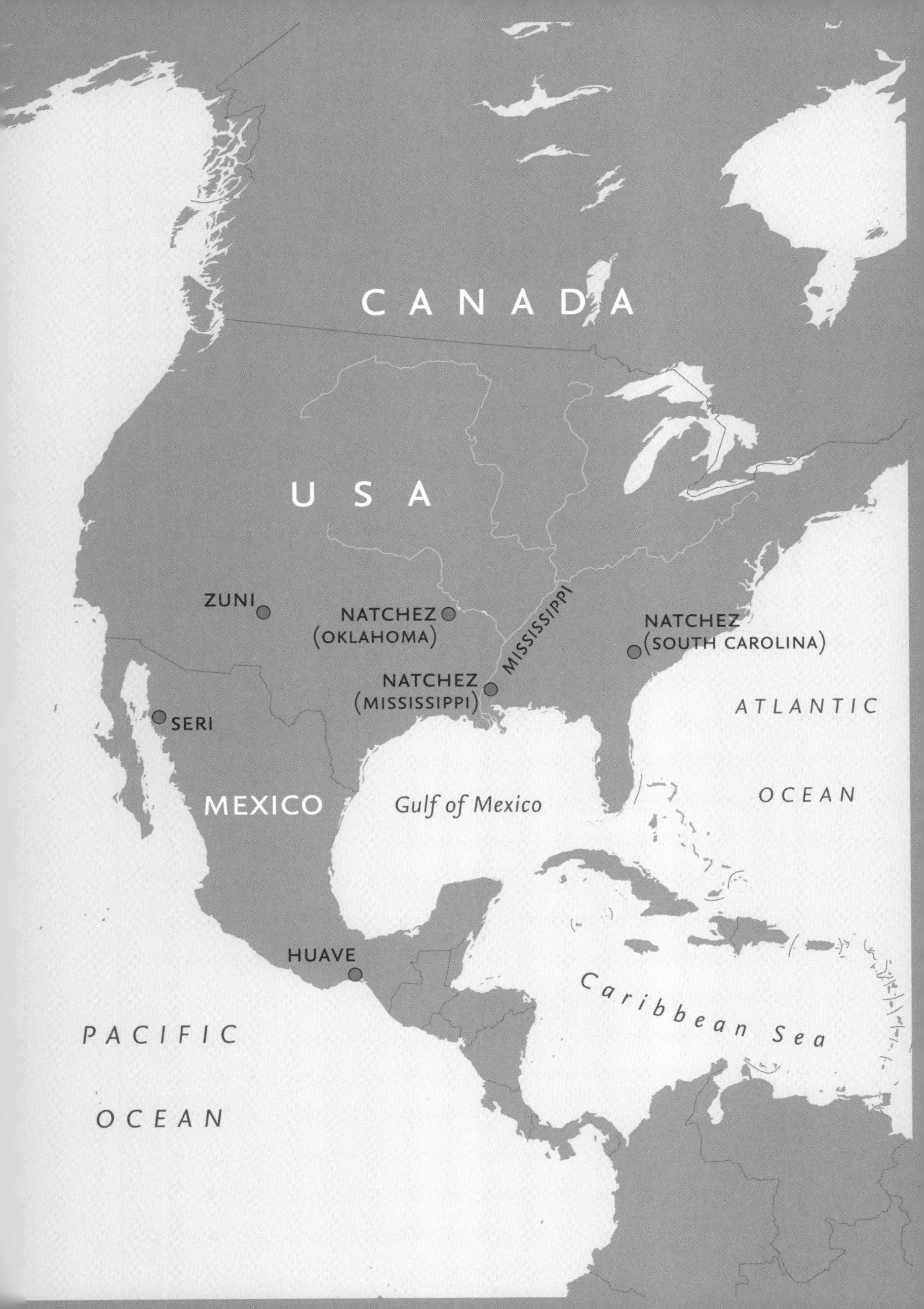

CANADA

USA

ZUNI

NATCHEZ
(OKLAHOMA)

NATCHEZ
(SOUTH CAROLINA)

MISSISSIPPI

NATCHEZ
(MISSISSIPPI)

SERI

MEXICO

Gulf of Mexico

ATLANTIC

OCEAN

HUAVE

Caribbean Sea

PACIFIC

OCEAN

SERI, MEXICO

Arabic, on the Pacific coast of Mexico? Yes, this was a recognized 'fun fact' in the middle of the nineteenth century, when the first list of words was compiled. And then, at the end of that century, someone realized that it was not an unusual dialect of Arabic that was being spoken, but **Seri**, a small indigenous language without any clearly confirmed connection with any other language in the world. The people who speak this language call themselves **Comcaac**, and their language **Cmiique iitom**; it is assumed that the word 'seri' comes from the language of one of the neighbouring tribes, although its meaning is not very clear. Today, a Seri population of approximately 1,000 inhabits two small towns on the Gulf Coast, **Punta Chueca** (**Socaaix** in Seri) and **El Desemboque** (**Haxöl Iihom** in Seri), where the language is still used extensively. Their community also includes the nearby islands in the Gulf of California, including **Tiburón Island**, a nature reserve and the largest Mexican island (1,200 square kilometres).

The language is relatively complicated, and has several interesting features: the number of terms used to denote relationships in the immediate and distant family is extremely large, so there are precise names for each family relationship, including for male and female in both directions (it matters whether someone is the grandson or granddaughter of his or her grandmother or grandfather). Another interesting fact is that new words are very rarely introduced for new terms, and instead standard expressions are used to describe a term or object. For example, in the Seri language, newspapers are *hapaspoj cmatsj*, which means 'paper that tells lies' (this term could be used in many other languages, right?), and radio is *ziix haa tiij coos* – 'the thing that stands there singing'.

HUAVE, MEXICO

On the Pacific coast of the narrowest part of Mexico – the Isthmus of Tehuantepec – not far from the city of Santo Domingo Tehuantepec, there is a large lagoon, and around it is the ancient land of the small community of **Huave**. Perhaps you are already thinking: members of this people speak the language isolate of **Huave (Wabe)**, which many scholars have been trying for decades to link to other indigenous languages of Mexico. For now, most linguists agree that it is a language isolate, and according to the legends of the Huave people, their ancestors came from Central America in ancient times. Four villages are home to about 18,000 Huave, of which nearly 12,000 speak their language. Each of these villages has its own dialect, although some linguists believe that these could each be viewed as a separate language within the Huave language family.

The Huave refer to themselves as 'we' (**Ikoots** or **Kunajts**, depending on the dialect), and call their speech 'our language' (**ombeayiiüts** or **umbeyajts**). The most active use of the language is in the village of **San Mateo del Mar**, where a large number of residents regularly use Huave in everyday speech. It has been noticed in all villages that the language is experiencing an unusual and unexpected revival; children and young people are learning certain words, phrases and basics of their ancestors' languages, so that they can interact on social media without the knowledge of their parents, who have completely switched to Spanish!

Bilingual Huave/Spanish welcome sign in San Mateo del Mar

ZUNI, USA

Just five kilometres from the border with Arizona in New Mexico, and some 300 kilometres west of the Grand Canyon, is **Zuni Pueblo**, a place with about 6,500 inhabitants. Of that number, approximately 95 per cent are members of the **Zuni** tribe (**A'shiwi** in Zuni), a people who speak another language isolate, the **Zuni**, locally known as **Shiwi'ma**. Despite considerable research, no related language has been found. This has not prevented the Zuni language from progressing for almost 7,000 years, although it has suffered great pressure from Spanish in the past, and from English today. According to sources, the Zuni language is regularly used today in households, religious ceremonies, on the radio and at tribal council meetings. It is estimated that there are about 9,500 speakers in Zuni Pueblo and its surroundings, as well as in a small area of Arizona. The fact that several primary and secondary schools are under the control of the Zuni tribe itself provides hope for the future of the language.

The main economic activity within the tribe's territory is agriculture, which employs an irrigation system that was developed about 3,000 years ago. Unique to this type of irrigation is the *waffle garden* (*Latdekwi'we* in Zuni), a field consisting of a network of squares, where each square is surrounded by a small embankment, so that all the water flows down to the middle of the square where the crops are.

Zuni waffle garden

NATCHEZ, USA

The problem with almost all 'small' languages is that they are threatened with extinction, with the last few speakers usually being assimilated into larger surrounding peoples or tribes. One such language is the isolated indigenous language of **Natchez** (with a silent 'z'), which officially became extinct in 1957 when Nancy Raven, the last person to speak the language fluently, died. Fortunately, numerous words, expressions and complete stories had been recorded both on paper and on wax cylinder, the precursor of gramophone records. This has enabled the gradual resurrection of the Natchez language, so that today there are officially at least six people who speak it fluently.

The Natchez people are the last descendants of the developed **Mississippian** culture, which existed in a large part of the Mississippi Valley from the ninth to the sixteenth centuries, and which the Natchez fully maintained until the eighteenth century. Their main deity was the Sun, and their community was arranged in the form of several castes, with one unusual twist: the rule was to always marry members of the highest and lowest castes.

Following several conflicts with the French and English colonies, a large number of Natchez were taken into slavery in the Caribbean, while most other members of the tribe were forcibly deported to Oklahoma. There, they joined a group called *Five Civilized Tribes*, made up of Cherokee, Muscogee (Creek), Chickasaw, Choctaw, and Seminole. Today, most of the Natchez live in the Cherokee Nation and Muscogee (Creek) Nation territories of **Oklahoma**. A small number remained on the land of their ancestors near the city of Natchez, **Mississippi**, the first capital of this state; also, in the state of **South Carolina**, in the valley of the Edisto river, there is a group of about 130 Natchez, a small number of whom know the basics of their language.

SOUTH AMERICA

Before the colonialization of South America, this continent was one of the most linguistically diverse areas on our planet, comparable to the island of New Guinea. The arrival, and often brutal rule, of European invaders – primarily the Portuguese and Spanish, and to a lesser extent the English, French and Dutch – and constant discrimination against the indigenous people led to the rapid disappearance of many languages. Still today, a large number of tribes, and their languages, are in danger of complete assimilation, and there is fear among linguists that South America could become linguistically very poor in the near future. According to current data, there are about 1,500 tribes in South America, although it is known that many of them do not have their own separate language. Nevertheless, there are at least 600 known indigenous languages, divided into approximately forty families. In addition to these languages and language families, South America is home to a large number of unclassified and language isolates.

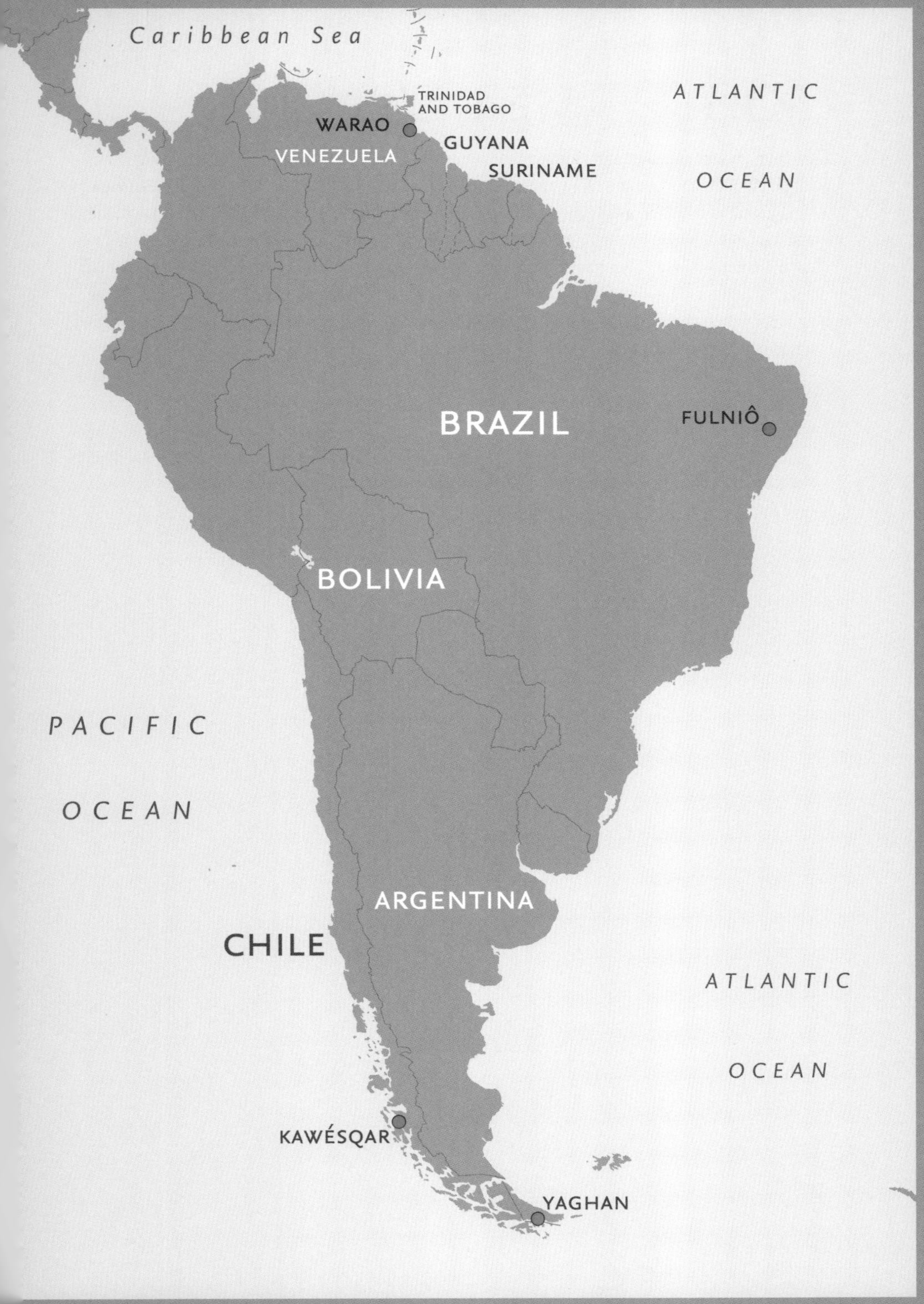

Caribbean Sea

ATLANTIC

OCEAN

TRINIDAD
AND TOBAGO

WARAO

VENEZUELA

GUYANA

SURINAME

BRAZIL

FULNIÔ

BOLIVIA

PACIFIC

OCEAN

ARGENTINA

CHILE

ATLANTIC

OCEAN

KAWÉSQAR

YAGHAN

FULNIÔ, BRAZIL

In the Brazilian state of **Pernambuco**, near the city of Águas Belas ('beautiful waters'), lies the home of the **Fulniô** tribe, the last speakers of an indigenous language in northwestern Brazil. Their language, **Fulniô** or **Ia-tê** ('our language'), is a language isolate, spoken by about 1,000 people, primarily the elderly. In everyday communication, Fulniô and **Portuguese** are used almost equally, but Fulniô is always used during the *Ouricuri* ritual. This ritual lasts from the end of August to October in a temporary location. Every adult Fulniô will try to attend the ritual for at least the first week, and everyone who is able will be present for all three months. The ritual itself is shrouded in secrecy, but it is known that people abstain from alcohol, music and sexual intercourse while in the 'ritual village' and that a shaman and chief of tribe is chosen.

The Fulniô language has numbers from 1 to 10, but today Portuguese numbers are usually used for 6 to 10, while compounds in the Fulniô language itself are less often used. For example, 6 can be translated as 'hand plus one'.

WARAO, VENEZUELA

Yoda, the little green humanoid from the *Star Wars* franchise, is famous for using an unusual word order in a sentence, so we can hear him say things like, 'Truly wonderful, the mind of a child is.' This arrangement of words in a sentence (object-subject-predicate; most languages usually use subject-predicate-object) may sound perfectly logical to speakers of about 0.3 per cent of the world's languages, including **Warao**. The **Warao** people have inhabited the **Orinoco River Delta** in northeastern Venezuela for thousands of years, but they have also spread to smaller parts of northern **Guyana**, the island of **Trinidad** and western **Suriname**. Most of the approximately 30,000 members of this nation regularly use their mother tongue, and they communicate without any problems with their compatriots from neighbouring countries. Unfortunately, the Warao language, also known as **Guarauno**, is barely studied in schools, which poses a risk to its future survival.

The houses of the Warao people are built on pillars above the water

YAGHAN AND KAWÉSQAR LANGUAGES, CHILE

In the extreme south of South America, three Fuegian tribes inhabit or used to inhabit **Tierra del Fuego** and parts of nearby **Patagonia** (today this area is divided between Chile and Argentina). Each of the tribes had its own language – **Yaghan** (**Yahgan, Yámana**), **Kawésqar** (**Qawasqar, Alacaluf**) and extinct **Chono** – which are, or were, language isolates. Today, the two languages that survive are extremely endangered, each only having a handful of speakers. Another Fuegian tribe, the **Selk'nam** (or **Ona**) tribe, were particularly affected by falling numbers, dropping from about 4,000 in the mid-nineteenth century to about 100 in the first half of the twentieth century. The rapid decline in their numbers was a result of the *Selk'nam genocide*, when almost the entire tribe was exterminated by settlers in a government-backed campaign.

Interestingly, there are scholars who claim that the Fuegians are not descendants of tribes that came to America from North Asia, but that their ancestors reached Patagonia by boat from Melanesia and the Pacific Ocean, which would make them the oldest inhabitants of America. Another interesting fact is related to the way the members of the Yaghan tribe dressed before they had contact with Europeans. Although these people inhabited areas with relatively cold climates, they were completely naked for most the time – they often even slept completely unprotected from the weather. They coated their bodies with large quantities of animal fat, and scientists today believe that over time they developed an extremely fast metabolism, which allowed their bodies to generate a greater amount of heat. It is known that they dived naked into cold sea waters to catch shellfish and other sea creatures.

'Ghosts' scare boys during hain, a ceremony in which boys become men

INDO-EUROPEAN LANGUAGE ISLANDS

SLAVIC LANGUAGE ISLANDS

The **Slavic** language family is the largest family in Europe. Its languages are spoken in much of Central and Eastern Europe, as well as in Southeast Europe, and North and Central Asia. There are approximately twenty Slavic languages which, together with several micro-languages, are generally divided into three groups: **East Slavic**, **West Slavic** and **South Slavic** languages.

BULGARIAN LANGUAGE ISLANDS

Bulgarians belong to the South Slavic ethnic group and inhabit Bulgaria and some of its neighbouring territories, with a large diaspora around the world. The modern Bulgarian nation was created by mixing several completely ethnically unconnected peoples and tribes (**Slavic** tribes, **Thracians** and **Turkic Bulgars**).

BANAT BULGARIANS IN ROMANIA AND SERBIA

Just near the Serbian–Romanian border (or **Banat** area) is the Romanian municipality of **Dudeştii Vechi**, or **Stár Bišnov** as it is known in the language of the majority ethnic community of **Banat Bulgarians** (**Palćene** in Banat Bulgarian). According to the 2011 census, the entire Dudeştii Vechi community has about 4,200 inhabitants, of which more than 60 per cent are Banat Bulgarian.

Banat Bulgarians speak a separate dialect of the Bulgarian language, characterized by a large number of loanwords from neighbouring languages (Romanian, Serbian, German and Hungarian). Unlike the Bulgarians from the motherland who write in **Cyrillic**, Banat Bulgarians use the adapted Serbo-Croatian **Latin alphabet**. Today, Banat Bulgarians live in Romania (numbering 6,500) and Serbia (about 1,500). Some Banat Bulgarian families have returned to their homeland, where they have settled several villages (Bardarski Geran, Dragomirovo and Asenovo) in the far north along the Danube River, receiving a new name: **Banaćani** ('people from Banat').

The main centres of Banat Bulgarian culture and language in Serbia are the villages of **Ivanovo** (out of 1,150 inhabitants, fewer than 30 per cent are Banat Bulgarian) and **Belo Blato** (8.5 per cent of the population). Ivanovo is located near Belgrade, the capital of Serbia.

An example of the difference between standard Bulgarian and Banat Bulgarian can be seen in a passage from the well-known book *The Little Prince*:

Standard Bulgarian (in Latin alphabet):
Ah, manichak printse, taka postepenno razbrah tvoya malak tazhen zhivot. Dalgo vreme edinstvenoto ti razvlechenie e bilo sladostta na slanchevite zalezi. Nauchih tazi nova podrobnost na chetvartiya den sutrinta, kogato ti mi kaza: Mnogo obicham slanchevite zalezi.

Banat Bulgarian:
O manani princ, léku pu léku iznamervami mananata tajnust na toja žuvot. Za dalgju vreme ni si se predstáveli udvanu na hubusta na zaseždenjétu na slancitu. I idna rabota détu sam ja iznamerili u ćtvartija denj sutirnata katu si mi ubadili: Tvarde mlogu mi harésva zaseždenjétu na slancitu.

BESSARABIAN BULGARIANS IN UKRAINE

The oppression suffered by subjects of the **Ottoman Empire** caused many to migrate to territories under Christian rule. One such migration took place during the late eighteenth and early nineteenth centuries, when a large number of Bulgarians and **Gagauz**[1] left their homes in the eastern part of Bulgaria, crossed the Danube and settled in the area between the Danube Delta and the Dniester river, called **Budzhak**[2].

These **Bessarabian Bulgarians** represent a significant national minority in Ukraine, with a population of about 205,000, of which almost 130,000 live in the Budzhak region. There are also 65,000 living in neighbouring Moldova.

The city of **Bolhrad** and the region around it represent the centre of the Bessarabian Bulgarians, who make up over 70 per cent of about 15,000 inhabitants. Bolhrad High School, founded in 1858, is considered one of the oldest Bulgarian high schools. The most important centre of the Bessarabian Bulgarians in Moldova is undoubtedly the southern city of **Taraclia**, where 78 per cent of the population is of Bulgarian origin. Bulgarians do not have any political autonomy within Moldova, unlike their Gagauz neighbours within the **Autonomous Territorial Unit of Gagauzia**.

Despite the large number of Bessarabian Bulgarians and other ethnic and linguistic minorities in Budzhak, the main language used in everyday communication is Russian.

---

[1] Gagauz are a Turkish people of the Eastern Orthodox religion, who today mostly inhabit Moldova, Ukraine and Turkey.

[2] The name 'Budzhak' originates from the time of the Ottoman rule (from the end of the fifteenth to the beginning of the nineteenth century), and comes from the Turkish word *bucak*, which means 'border area'.

SERBIAN AND MONTENEGRIN LANGUAGE ISLANDS

The historical, religious and linguistic ties of **Serbs** and **Montenegrins** are extremely strong, and **Serbian** and **Montenegrin** languages are completely mutually intelligible. Serbs inhabit Slovenia (several villages in the region of Bela Krajina, known as White Carniola) and North Macedonia (the villages of Marvinci, Crničani, Selemli – Selemlija in Serbian – and Nikolik), but here we will visit their settlements in Hungary, Albania and Romania.

SERBS IN HUNGARY

The migrations of Serbs during the Ottoman conquests led to the formation of Serbian language islands within Hungarian territory. Serbs in Hungary are a recognized national minority, officially numbering just over 7,000 people. Today, in Hungary, there is only one place with a majority Serb population, the village of **Lórév** (**Lovra** in Serbian), located about 50 kilometres south of Budapest, making it the northernmost Serbian settlement. Of the approximately 310 inhabitants, almost 60 per cent are Orthodox Serb and the rest are Hungarian.

There are a few other settlements near Lórév where a small number of Serbs live. The town of **Ráckeve** (**Srpski Kovin** in Serbian) has 10,000 inhabitants, of which several hundred are Serb. This town is characterized by the fact that it has probably the only Serbian church built in the Gothic style, dating from 1448.

The interior of the Serbian monastery in Ráckeve (Srpski Kovin)

MONTENEGRINS IN CROATIA

Peroj is a small place in the south of Istria, the largest Croatian peninsula. The story of the Montenegrins and Peroj begins in the middle of the sixteenth century. When the population of Istria was decimated by the plague and malaria, the authorities of the Republic of Venice resettled Peroj in 1657 with twenty-five Eastern Orthodox families from near Lake Skadar (also known as Lake Scutari) – which lies on what is now the border of Montenegro and Albania – who were fleeing Turkish oppression. Descendants of these families have remained in Peroj to this day, preserving their faith, customs and language throughout the centuries, including through some extremely difficult periods.

SERBS IN ALBANIA

Serbs in Albania have lived in the territory for centuries, as evidenced by the numerous Slavic names of geographical features. They are concentrated primarily in the northern part, near Lake Skadar and the border with Montenegro. However, 150 kilometres southwest of the capital Tirana are the villages of **Hamil** and **Libofshë**, inhabited by large numbers of Serbs (unofficial figures put the number between 100 and 2,000). These Serbs originate from the north of Albania, from where they moved to the vicinity of Fier, the second largest Albanian city, at the beginning of the twentieth century.

The life of these Serbian immigrants was very difficult during the rule of Enver Hoxha, with a complete ban on the use of language and any national symbols. Today, the situation is somewhat better: a Serbian school teaching Serbian language, culture and history recently opened in Hamil and is attended by sixty children.

It is interesting to note that in the nineteenth century, a Serb from Albania, Đorđe Berović (George Berovich in English, Beroviç Paşa in Turkish), reached high positions within the Ottoman Empire, being governor of Crete for some time, and then ruler of the semi-independent state of the Principality of Samos.

SERBS IN ROMANIA

Northeast of today's Serbia, in the area of Romanian Banat, there are two areas in which several Serbian language islands exist. The first area is known as **Clisura Dunării** or **Defileul Dunării** (**Banatska klisura** in Serbian: 'Banat gorge') and includes the Romanian side of the Danube. The names of a large number of settlements, rivers and hills are of Slavic origin, which is evidence that Slavs (mostly Serbs) represent one of the oldest ethnic groups in this region. The villages of **Svinița** (**Svinjica** in Serbian), **Socol** (**Sokolovac** in Serbian; birthplace of Miodrag Belodedić or Belodedici, one of the best football players in the world) and **Pojejena** (**Požežena** in Serbian) are the last villages with a Serbian majority in the area of the Banat gorge. The bilingual village of Svinița/Svinjica is inhabited by about 950 people; over 90 per cent of the population is Serb.

The second area is called **Banatska Crna Gora** in Serbian ('black mountain of Banat'), and is located about a hundred kilometres from the border with Serbia, between the cities of Timișoara and Lugoj. After the end of the First World War and the disintegration of the **Austro-Hungarian Empire**, the entire region belonged to Romania. This accelerated the immigration of Romanians from the regions of Wallachia and Moldavia, and in time only four villages remained with a Serb ethnic majority.

Of all the villages in Banatska Crna Gora, **Cralovăț** (**Kraljevac** in Serbian) has probably the highest percentage of ethnic Serbs, making up 80 per cent of the 200 inhabitants. To the west of Cralovăț is **Petrovaselo** (**Petrovo Selo** in Serbian), while to the east is the village of **Lucareț** (**Lukarevac** in Serbian). Lucareț/Lukarevac is first mentioned in 1492, the same year that Christopher Columbus reached America. One building especially singles out the village: the church of St George is the oldest Serbian parish church in Romania.

The old Serbian church in Lucareț/Lukarevac

'GREAT SPRING' LANGUAGE, SERBIA AND BULGARIA

Three villages in the Balkan region stand out: the villages of **Golyam Izvor** in Bulgaria, and **Veliki Izvor** and **Dublje** in Serbia. What connects these three villages is a specific language, which the locals have been speaking for centuries.

Their story begins in the thirteenth century, when the **Mongol** invasion completely destroyed then-Russian principalities, causing enormous damage to the large cities of Vladimir, Moscow and Kiev. Georgi Glozh, the prince of Kievan Rus', fled from Kiev to Bulgaria where Tsar Ivan Asen II gave him land near the town of Teteven to build monasteries and villages. This area was initially called Kievski Izvor, later renamed Golyam Izvor (the Bulgarian translated into English means 'great spring').

In the middle of the eighteenth century, a large group of residents of the village of Golyam Izvor (known as **Tetevenci** after the town of Teteven) left their homes and headed to the town of Zaječar, not far from today's Serbian–Bulgarian border. This group inhabited the abandoned village of Stupanj, which was connected with the neighbouring villages of Alapin and Izvor, thus forming the village of Veliki Izvor (the Serbian translated into English means 'great spring').

At the end of the eighteenth century, some of the inhabitants of Veliki Izvor decided to build a new village near the present-day town of Svilajnac. They allegedly occupied a forest, which they slowly cleared and advanced deeper into, and so the village was named Dublje, meaning 'deeper' in English.

To various degrees, the inhabitants of these villages still use the language that many describe as a mixture of Bulgarian, Serbian and Macedonian. However, many linguists believe that the language in question is largely independent of the known South Slavic languages, and could be regarded as another independent language on the Balkan Peninsula.

The physical isolation of Veliki Izvor also resulted in linguistic isolation, so that even today a significant number of inhabitants still use the **'Great Spring'** language, although Veliki Izvor is now a suburb of the city of Zaječar. The situation in Dublje is a bit worse, with fewer and fewer people using the language of their ancestors. But despite the great geographical distance between these three villages, their inhabitants can still understand each other without any problems.

LANGUAGE ISLANDS IN VOJVODINA, SERBIA

Vojvodina is an autonomous province within the Republic of Serbia. It occupies northern Serbia and consists of three physical-geographical areas: Srem (Syrmia), Bačka and Banat. This area of about 21,600 square kilometres (slightly larger than Israel) is home to two million citizens, representing more than twenty-five ethnic groups, and speaking several dozen languages, six of which have official status throughout the territory (**Serbian**, **Hungarian**, **Romanian**, **Slovak**, **Rusyn** and **Croatian**). A large number of languages are used within the local authorities. So many languages in a relatively small area make Vojvodina a *linguistic archipelago*!

LANGUAGE ISLANDS OF THE PANNONIAN RUTHENIANS

Pannonian Ruthenians (**Rusyns**), numbering 20,000, represent one of the smaller Slavic peoples. Today, they mostly inhabit parts of western Vojvodina, with several settlements in Bačka and Srem. Ruthenians have been living in Vojvodina since 1751, when the Austro-Hungarian Empress Maria Theresa took the decision to resettle Ruthenian Greek Catholic families in Bačka, from the area around the present-day border of Ukraine, Slovakia and Poland.

   Ruski Krstur (**Ruski Kerestur** in Rusyn: 'Rusyn (place of the) cross') is the main cultural and national centre of the Pannonian Ruthenians. This village has about 5,500 inhabitants, over 85 per cent of whom are Ruthenians, though this number is constantly declining due to emigration, primarily to the city of North Battleford, Saskatchewan, Canada. Only 15 kilometres from Ruski Krstur is **Kucura** (**Kocur** in Rusyn), another place inhabited by a large number of Ruthenians (accounting for almost half of the 4,600 inhabitants).

   The primary school in **Kucura** is attended by 400 students, who have classes in Ruthenian or Serbian. In 2013, the inhabitants of Kucura celebrated 250 years since the Ruthenians moved to this village, and every year several important cultural and artistic events are held.

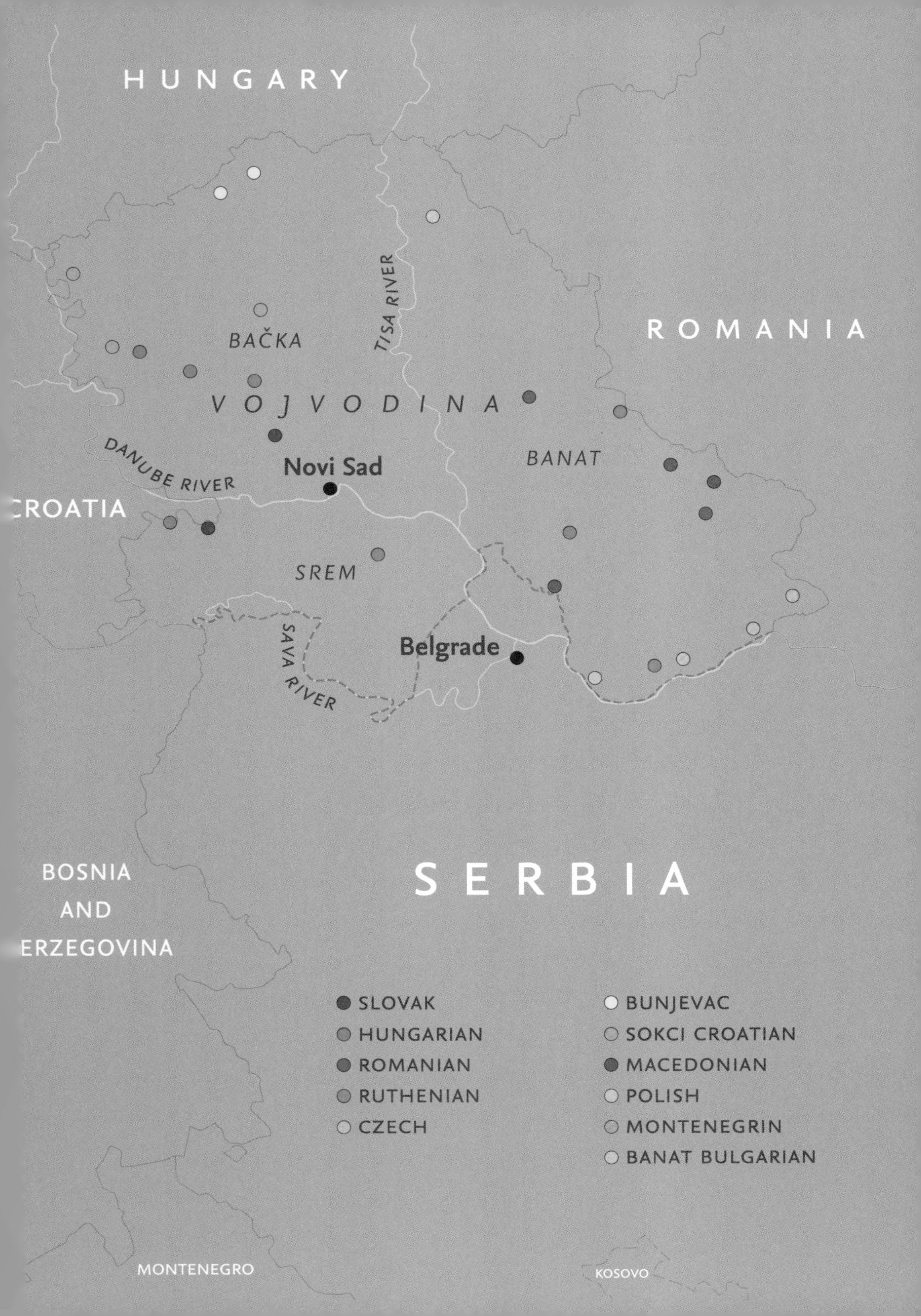

HUNGARY

ROMANIA

TISA RIVER

BAČKA

VOJVODINA

BANAT

DANUBE RIVER

Novi Sad

CROATIA

SREM

Belgrade

SAVA RIVER

BOSNIA
AND
HERZEGOVINA

SERBIA

MONTENEGRO

KOSOVO

- ● SLOVAK
- ● HUNGARIAN
- ● ROMANIAN
- ● RUTHENIAN
- ○ CZECH
- ○ BUNJEVAC
- ○ SOKCI CROATIAN
- ● MACEDONIAN
- ○ POLISH
- ○ MONTENEGRIN
- ○ BANAT BULGARIAN

CZECH LANGUAGE ISLANDS

The **Czechs** are a West Slavic people living primarily in Czechia (Czech Republic), with a smaller number also living in northern Serbia.

With fewer than fifty inhabitants, **Češko Selo** (Serbian for 'Czech village') is probably the smallest village in Vojvodina, and the only place in the whole of Serbia with a Czech majority. Czech organizations in Serbia are making great efforts to attract tourists to Češko Selo, and since 2007 the *Paprikašijada* ('festival of paprikaš dish') has been held regularly.

The village of **Kruščica** is located not far from Češko Selo, on the border with Romania. A total of 860 people live in Kruščica, of which the Czechs make up slightly less than a quarter, while Serbs make up nearly three-quarters.

MACEDONIAN LANGUAGE ISLANDS

More than 22,000 **Macedonians** inhabit Serbia, primarily Vojvodina and Belgrade. **Jabuka** ('apple'; 6,500 inhabitants) is a village located on the inner border of Vojvodina and the city of Belgrade, only 15 kilometres from the centre of the capital. The first Macedonians immigrated immediately after the end of the Second World War, but Serbs remained the majority population, so that today one third of the population of Jabuka belongs to the Macedonian people, and half to the Serbians. The biggest Macedonian holiday, *Ilinden*, is regularly celebrated in Jabuka and other Macedonian settlements (**Plandište** and **Dužine**) in Vojvodina. In all of the Macedonian settlements mentioned here, the official use of the **Macedonian** language and script is allowed.

SLOVAK LANGUAGE ISLANDS

Slovaks are primarily Catholic in Slovakia, Protestant in Serbia. Both groups of Slovaks speak **Slovak**, one of the West Slavic languages and one of the six official languages of Vojvodina. The ancestors of most of today's Slovaks from Vojvodina emigrated during the eighteenth and nineteenth centuries from what is now the border area of Slovakia and Hungary.

Bački Petrovac (**Báčsky Petrovec** in Slovak) is a town of about 7,500 inhabitants, located in the southern part of Bačka; it is the economic, cultural and political centre of the Bačka Slovaks. Slovaks make up more than 80 per cent of the city's population, so it's no wonder that it houses the Slovak school and the Museum of Vojvodina Slovaks.

Forty kilometres from Belgrade, in the southern part of Banat, is **Kovačica**, a town that has gained world renown as the centre of Slovak naïve art, which is represented by Zuzana Chalupová, Martin Jonas, Jan Sokol, Jan Glozik and many more.

Two hundred years of Kovačica (Jan Glozik)

POLES IN SERBIA

A few hundred **Poles** from **Ostojićevo**, a village located in the north of Serbia, are the descendants of miners from around the town of Wisła in southern Poland, not far from the tripoint with Czechia (Czech Republic) and Slovakia. In search of a better life, the miners started moving to the Ostojićevo area (then known as Tiszaszentmiklós, 'Saint Nicholas on the Tisza') in the middle of the nineteenth century, where they extracted saltpetre, which was used in the production of gunpowder. They brought with them their evangelical faith, as well as the local dialect of the Polish language, known as the **Silesian** language or dialect. Although few in number, the Poles of Vojvodina have kept their vernacular, today full of archaic forms, which in the meantime have disappeared from the language of the mother country.

Polish cultural and artistic society from Ostojićevo in Wisła, 2019

GORANI/NAŠINSKI LANGUAGE OF GORA

Gorani are a separate Slavic people, whose members are followers of the Islamic faith. They speak their own independent **Gorani** language (which is close to other **Torlakian** dialects) and have some customs which were inherited from the period before the adoption of Islam.

Most Gorani live south of Prizren in an area known as **Gora** (**Gorë** in Albanian), which includes eighteen villages in Kosovo*, nine villages in Albania and two in North Macedonia. There are thought to be about 60,000 Gorani (although some sources claim there are actually fewer than 30,000), of which a third live in Gora, and the remaining two-thirds in the diaspora. The name 'Gorani' comes from the Slavic word *gora* ('mountain') and means 'people who live in the mountains'. They most often call themselves **Našinci**, which is an expression that comes from the Slavic word *naši*, meaning 'our (people)'. From that name comes the common

*Kosovo is recognized as an independent country by the UK, USA, most European Union member countries and just over half of all UN members. Many other countries do not recognize it, including Serbia, Russia and China.

name for the language, which Gorani usually call **Našinski**, 'our (language)'. This language is obviously South Slavic, with a large number of words borrowed from Turkish and Arabic (a consequence of belonging to Islam), and from the Albanian language (a consequence of the geographical position of Gora, which is mostly surrounded by Albanian villages).

Today, there are noticeable attempts by all surrounding South Slavic countries to attract Gorani into their national and ethnic being, in order to assimilate them. Albanians are trying to do the same, and at the last census in North Macedonia, most Gorani in two Gorani villages declared themselves as Turks.

Under the influence of the Ottoman Turks, a large number of Gorani accepted Islam in the eighteenth century; some Gorani still celebrate some of the Christian customs, such as St George's Day and the celebration of the family's patron saint.

Gorani still often adhere to the old custom of building the *ayret fountain*. These fountains are usually made in memory of a deceased person or as a gift to all passers-by. This custom may be based on the scarcity of water in the past, making these fountains very useful structures.

Ayret fountain near Restelicë (Restelica in Serbian), the largest village in Gora

BOSNIAK LANGUAGE ISLANDS IN ALBANIA AND TURKEY

BOSNIAKS IN ALBANIA

When the predominantly Catholic Austro-Hungarians occupied Bosnia and Herzegovina at the end of the nineteenth century, some of the **Bosniaks** from Herzegovina, loyal to the Turkish sultan, decided to seek their happiness in Turkey. According to the story, a large number of families boarded a ship that was supposed to take them to Turkey, but which broke down near Durrës, a port on the southern Adriatic Sea. While waiting for the ship to be repaired, the Bosniaks noticed the river nearby and the valley around it, which reminded them of the surroundings of the Neretva river in Herzegovina, from where they had set off. When they realized that the ship repairs would take some time, they decided to settle in this area between Durrës and Tirana, today's capital of Albania.

The inhabiting Bosniaks founded the villages of **Borakë** and **Koxhas**, and their descendants still form the majority population. The village of Borakë is almost exclusively Bosniak, while the population of neighbouring Koxhas is ethnically mixed; today, 7,000 Bosniaks live in the entire municipality to which these villages belong. During their century-and-a-half-long stay in Albania, there has been very little conflict between the Bosniaks and Albanians, primarily due to the common faith, but also the fact that Bosniaks are considered hardworking and honest people. Despite this, the status of a national minority was granted to them only in 2017.

BOSNIAKS IN TURKEY

Some groups of Bosniaks still managed to reach Turkey, and according to some estimates, there are significantly more of them in that country than there are in their home country of Bosnia and Herzegovina. A large number of them have completely assimilated and today regard themselves as Turks. However, in several villages, Bosniaks continue to use their Slavic language regularly, maintain all their customs and have a sense of belonging to the Bosniak people. Unfortunately, the use of the **Bosnian** language (sometimes called **Bosniak** language) is not allowed in schools, and it is usually mandatory to change the surname to one that sounds more Turkish.

The village of **Turanköy** is located not far from the shores of the Sea of Marmara and the city of Bursa. Most of the elderly inhabitants speak Bosnian, with frequent loanwords from modern Turkish as well as Ottoman Turkish. Young people are using the language of their ancestors less and less and are rapidly switching to Turkish. Just 30 kilometres from the Turkish capital of Ankara is another old Bosniak village, **Fevziye**, with nearly 2,000 Bosniaks. This place is known for *Pie Day*, a competitive celebration, where the goal is to make the best Bosnian pie, of which there are several well-known varieties. In the Asian part of Istanbul province, just a few kilometres from the Black Sea coast, approximately 450 Bosniaks live in the village of **Yeniköy**, known for producing excellent chestnut honey. Bosniaks moved to the village of **Aksicim** between the two world wars, and they still speak their language, which they usually call Bosniak. There is a danger of assimilation, with young people increasingly leaving this village, and those who remain increasingly switching to Turkish.

CROATIAN LANGUAGE ISLANDS

CROATS IN ROMANIA

In the picturesque hilly landscape close to the Semenic-Caraș Gorge National Park, 20 kilometres from the Romanian–Serbian state border, are the towns of **Carașova** (**Kraševo** in the local Slavic dialect) and **Lupac** (**Lupak** in Croatian), where the majority of inhabitants regard themselves as ethnic **Croats** and speak the **Croatian** language. These two places are the westernmost settlements with a majority Croat population. Until the end of the twentieth century, the inhabitants of Carașova and Lupac mostly considered themselves **Kraševani** (**Kraševci**), without any special ethnic identification. The origin of the Kraševani is not clearly established, but three areas stand out as possible locations from which the ancestors of this community came: the Turopolje area not far from the Croatian capital of Zagreb, northwestern Bosnia and Herzegovina, or the southeastern part of Serbia.

It is apparent that the people of Carașova are slowly but surely losing their archaic Torlakian speech and are increasingly switching to the use of the standard Croatian language. The reason for this is simple: most Catholic priests in Carașova and Lupac are sent from Croatia, which also provides textbooks for Kraševani schools.

CROATS IN AUSTRIA AND HUNGARY

Around the end of the fifteenth century, a group of Croats fled from the Ottoman Empire. The area where they settled among Hungarians was known as **Western Hungary**; those whose mother tongue was German call this area **Burgenland**, while in Croatian it is called **Gradišće**. After the name of this area and today's easternmost Austrian federal province, this South Slavic ethnic group was named **Burgenland Croats**. Burgenland was a poor and relatively isolated area, enabling the Croats to preserve their specific language, which has even progressed in recent times. Many villages and towns in this area still bear names of Slavic origin. For example, the village of Parndorf near Vienna is named after Perun, the supreme Slavic deity. According to available data, in Burgenland about 20–30,000 people regularly use the **Burgenland Croatian** language, as an officially accepted variant of the Croatian language.

Burgenland Croats also live in several small towns in Hungary along the border with Austria.

Let us compare some Croatian language variants using a passage from *The Little Prince*:

Standard Croatian:
Ah! mali prinče, tako sam polako počinjao razumijevati tvoj mali melankolični život. Dugo si vremena za razonodu imao samo ljepotu sunčevih zalazaka. To sam doznao ujutro četvrtog dana kada si mi rekao: Vrlo mi se sviđaju zalasci sunca.

Burgenland Croatian:
Ah! Mali prinče, tako sam lipo polako razumio tvoj mali, turobni žitak. Dugo vrime je samo lipota zahadjanja sunca bila tvoja jedina zabav. Tu novu pojedinost sam doznao četvrti dan jutro, kada si mi rekao: Ljubim zahadjanja sunca.

Molisano Croatian:
A! Mali kraljič, ja sa razumija, na mala na votu, naka, tvoj mali život malingonik. Ti s'bi jima sa čuda vrima kana dištracijunu sama ono slako do sutanji. Ja sa znaja ovu malu aš novu stvaru, dòp četar dana jistru, kada ti s'mi reka: Su mi čuda drage sutanja.

CROATS IN ITALY

Some Slavs from the Balkans believed it would be safest to flee from the Ottomans by boat to the southern part of the Italian 'boot'. It is assumed that the first **Catholic Slavs** left the Dalmatian coast of the Adriatic Sea and that they reached the surroundings of the city of Bari by boat from the Neretva valley at the end of the fifteenth century. It is known that in 1497, near the town of Gioia del Colle, together with other subjects, they welcomed Isabella del Balzo, Queen of Naples, to whom they sang in their language, *Orao se vijaše nad gradom Smederevom* ('An eagle glided over the town of Smederevo'), the oldest recorded *bugarštica*, a once popular type of epic folk song of Dalmatia and Boka Kotorska.

Some believe that at the time, southern Italy was inhabited by several thousand Slavs, distributed in about fifteen villages and towns. However, it is only in three villages that relative isolation has helped to preserve the language and customs, although most of the inhabitants' names have been Italianized and the population is declining constantly. These villages are located in the Adriatic region of **Molise**, hence the name for this Slavic dialect: **Slavomolisano**.

The largest village inhabited by **Molise Croats** is **Acquaviva Collecroce** (**Kruč** in the local Croatian dialect), followed by **San Felice del Molise** (**Filič**) and **Montemitro** (**Mundimitar**); all three villages have separate dialects. Today, a total of about 2,000 Molise Croats live in these villages, with only half of them speaking their mother tongue.

For a long time – practically from their immigration to the Apennine Peninsula until the beginning of the twentieth century – Molise Slavs had almost no sense of nationality or the name of their language. They call their language **na našo** ('in our language') and they do not have a special name for themselves, although they often use the term **Škjavuna**, which is an old Italian form of the word 'Slavs'.

Fešta do Maja in the village of Kruč — a popular celebration of the arrival of May and spring

RESIAN IN ITALY

The average Slovenian from Slovenia or Italy would have major trouble understanding their compatriots living in the small **Resia Valley**, just a few kilometres from the Slovenian border. The small population of this valley, a little less than 2,000, speaks an unusual dialect of the **Slovenian** language, known as the **Resian** dialect or **rozajanski langač**, as they call it. This dialect contains a number of unusual characteristics, significantly different from any other dialect of the Slovenian language. Numerous archaisms have been retained, and many letters that do not exist in the Slovenian language are used, such as vowels with umlauts, the letter 'ć', and also 'w', which is used in only a few Slavic languages. Some linguists believe that the use of the letter 'w' is a clear indicator of the great influence of **Ladin** and other **Rhaeto-Romance** languages on this Slavic language. The presence of a large number of loanwords of **Romance** origin also supports this opinion. All this is the reason why many speakers of Resian believe that it is an independent language, and not merely a dialect of Slovenian. Apart from their specific speech, the inhabitants of the Resia Valley are also known for their extremely imaginative stories, as well as their energetic dances and unusual folk music with hints of Celtic melodies.

The names of the months are a good example of the differences between Resian and standard Slovenian:

RESIAN	SLOVENIAN	ENGLISH
ĞANAR	JANUAR	JANUARY
FAVRAR	FEBRUAR	FEBRUARY
MÄRČ	MAREC	MARCH
AVRÏL	APRIL	APRIL
MÄJ	MAJ	MAY
JONJ	JUNIJ	JUNE
ŽUŽLUDÖR	JULIJ	JULY
AVOŠT	AVGUST	AUGUST
SETEMBAR	SEPTEMBER	SEPTEMBER
OTOBAR	OKTOBER	OCTOBER
NOVEMBAR	NOVEMBER	NOVEMBER
DIČEMBAR	DECEMBER	DECEMBER

These striking hats are part of the folk costume from the Resia Valley, Italy

SORBIAN LANGUAGES

The **Lusatia** region (**Łužyca** in Lower Sorbian, **Łužica** in Upper Sorbian, **Lausitz** in German) is located on the border of Poland, Czechia (Czech Republic) and Germany. The largest part of the region belongs to Germany, with about 60,000 **Sorbs**, or **Wends**, living there. Sorbs are Western Slavic people linguistically divided into speakers of **Upper Sorbian** (close to Czech) and **Lower Sorbian** (close to Polish). The two groups of Sorbs were separated for centuries by dense forests and swamps, so the differences between their languages increased.

West and East Germany were united in 1990. This led to the improvement of the status of Sorbs, but still their greatest wish was not realized – the establishment of Lusatia as one of the German federal states.

Today, there are several smaller places where Sorbs represent the majority, while in larger places they make up a much smaller percentage. The population of the main centre of Upper Lusatia (which is the southern part of the region), the town of **Bautzen** (**Budyšin** in Upper Sorbian), today has less than 10 per cent Sorbs, but almost all national and cultural institutions of this Slavic people are located there.

The differences between the two standard forms of the Sorbian language are illustrated in this passage from *The Little Prince*:

Upper Sorbian:
Ach, mały princo, poněčim sym twoje małe ćežkomyslne žiwjenčko zrozumił ... Dołho njejsy hinašeho rozwjeselenja měł, hač lubozne chowanje słónca. To zhonich štwórty dźeń rano, jako sy mi prajił: Chowanje słónca přewšo lubuju.

Lower Sorbian:
Och, mały princ! Pózlažka som rozměł twójo melancholiske žywjenje. Dotychměst sy rozwjaselenje jano měł nad chowanim słyńca. Som to akle na stwórtem dnju žajtša zgónił, ako sy ku mnjo gronił: Ja lubuju to wujźenje słyńca.

In the middle of the nineteenth century, about 2,000 Sorbs emigrated to the Australian **Barossa Valley**, 30 kilometres north of Adelaide. The Sorbian language is no longer used there, but several associations observe certain traditions of their ancestors. At the same time, a group of about 600 Sorbs settled in central Texas, United States, where they formed the town of **Serbin**, which houses the Texas Wendish Heritage Museum. It is possible that there are still several speakers of the Sorbian language in the very centre of The Lone Star State.

Sorbs celebrate Easter with a traditional horse parade

AND A FEW MORE SLAVIC LANGUAGE ISLANDS...

POLES IN TURKEY

During the nineteenth century, Russia, Austria and Prussia divided the territory of Poland between them. A Polish rebellion was defeated in 1831, after which two gathering centres were organized for **Polish** emigrants, one in Paris and the other in Turkey.

A place on the Asian side of the Bosporus river, some 30 kilometres away from the centre of Istanbul, was chosen as the location of the Polish centre in Turkey. There, in 1842, a village was formed, which the Turks named **Polonezköy** ('Polish village'), and which the settled Poles called **Adampol**. There is still a Polish Catholic church in Adampol, and the descendants of immigrant Poles maintain their customs, festivals and dances. Out of about 400 inhabitants, Poles make up a third of the population, but only about fifty of them still regularly use the **Polish** language in communication with family and friends.

KASHUBIAN, POLAND

Kashubian is spoken on a stretch of the Polish coast, mostly between the lower reaches of the Vistula and Oder rivers, in an area **Kashubians** call **Kaszëbë**. Of the approximately 200,000 people who know this language, just over half use it daily. Since 2005, Kashubian has had the status of an ethnic minority language in Poland. Linguistic research has shown that the Kashubian language is the only living successor of the extinct **Pomeranian** language, spoken by members of the West Slavic tribes on the Baltic coast of today's Poland.

A large number of Kashubians and Poles emigrated to Canada in the middle of the nineteenth century, where they populated many existing settlements and founded new ones; one such settlement was **Wilno**, Ontario. Kashubian and Polish culture and customs are still very much alive in this part of Canada, together with popular folk events – *Wilno Chicken Supper* and *Kashub Day Festival* are two of them – that are attended even by people who do not have Kashubian or Polish origins.

The **Slovincian** language (**Słowińskô mòwa**) was the closest relative of the Kashubian language (or its dialect), and was spoken by the **Slovincians** until the beginning of the twentieth century. The Slovincians usually called themselves **Lebski Kashubi**, Leba being a river that flows through northern Poland. Today, several dozen Slovincians still live in the village of **Kluki** (**Kláhi** in Slovincian, **Klëczi** in Kashubian), using only a few phrases from the language of their ancestors. There is a Slovincian open-air museum in Kluki, and fascinating moving sand dunes can be seen nearby in Słowiński National Park.

RUSSIAN LANGUAGE ISLANDS

An agreement was signed in Paris in 1920 recognizing the sovereignty of Norway over the **Svalbard** archipelago, but guaranteeing the rights of fishing, hunting and exploitation of mineral resources to all signatory countries (fourteen initially, now forty-six). For now, only Norway and Russia use that right. Svalbard is a completely demilitarized area, for which no one needs a visa or work permit.

The town of **Barentsburg** is a Russian mining town on the island of Spitsbergen, inhabited by about 450 Russians and Ukrainians. At the time of greatest prosperity, the number of inhabitants of the town reached about 1,000. Not far from Barentsburg is **Pyramiden**, a Soviet ghost mining town, which closed in 1998 when coal mining was discontinued. Due to the cold climate of Svalbard, a large number of buildings have remained almost intact, making Pyramiden quite a popular tourist destination for ships passing through the area; the village is now home to several **Russians** who maintain the hotel and take care of the tourists.

When the Russian Patriarch Nikon began reforming the Russian Orthodox Church in the middle of the seventeenth century, some believers rebelled and formed a religious group based on old beliefs, and became known as the **Old Believers**. A large number of these believers retreated to hard-to-reach areas of Siberia, then fled to China, later to the São Paulo area of Brazil, and after a while to Oregon, United States, on their way north to Alaska. In 1968 they founded several settlements in Kenai Peninsula Borough, 150 kilometres south of Anchorage. These villages (**Nikolaevsk**, **Voznesenka**, **Razdolna** and **Kachemak Selo**) are still mostly inhabited by Russians, who have their churches and restaurants serving national food. A large number of people still speak **Russian**, although this applies to a decreasing number of young people.

Another group of Russian Old Believers decided to seek refuge in the Danube Delta, where they are known as **Lipovans** (probably derived from Slavic word for 'linden' – *lipa*). Around the Danube Delta, they are found in a number of villages, such as **Carcaliu**, where Lipovans make up 90 per cent of the 2,500 inhabitants. In Ukraine, the main Lipovan settlement is **Vylkove** (8,000 inhabitants, 70 per cent Lipovan), also known as the *Venice of Ukraine*, due to the large number of canals in the village, which are often used as streets. Lipovans speak the old Russian language, which has retained many features of the language from the seventeenth and eighteenth centuries.

Some members of other Russian religious groups were simply expelled to the outskirts of the former **Russian Empire**. One such group, known as **Spiritual Christians**, were expelled by the Russian authorities in the middle of the nineteenth century to Armenia, where they settled in two villages, **Fioletovo** (1,000 inhabitants) and **Lermontovo** (800 inhabitants).

Russian Orthodox church in Barentsburg, Svalbard

UKRAINIANS IN REPUBLIKA SRPSKA, BOSNIA AND HERZEGOVINA

Groups of **Ukrainians** from the area of Galicia (western Ukraine and southeastern Poland) settled in the northern parts of Bosnia and Herzegovina after the Austro-Hungarians occupied Bosnia in 1878. Today, Ukrainians are mostly settled in the northern parts of Republika Srpska, where they represent the majority population in several small towns. Despite their small number, Ukrainians have preserved their language, customs and culture. Probably the main settlement of the Bosnian Ukrainians is the village of **Devetina**, where about a hundred Ukrainians still live. The village still uses a somewhat archaic form of the **Ukrainian** language, and the church is a place of pilgrimage for all Ukrainians from the former **Yugoslavia**. Near the church there is a forest with nine large stones, from which the village took its name (*devet* = nine).

BALTIC LANGUAGE ISLANDS

The **Baltic** languages belong to the Baltic-Slavic branch of the Indo-Eurpoean language tree. They are divided into **Western** (which are all now extinct) and **Eastern**, whose two surviving languages are **Latvian** and **Lithuanian**, including their variants. Baltic languages are considered to be very conservative languages, with Lithuanian being the most conservative living Indo-European language. This means that the Lithuanian language has retained the most features of the long-lost Proto-Indo-European language. The **Samogitian** language (**žemaitiu kalba** in Samogitian) is an Eastern Baltic language or dialect of the Lithuanian language, spoken by several hundred thousand people in **Samogitia**, the westernmost part of Lithuania. **Kursenieki** language (**kursisk valuod**) is a Latvian dialect spoken by fewer than a dozen people on the sandy **Curonian Spit**, divided by Lithuania and Russia.

LATGALIAN

Latgalian is an Eastern Baltic language, spoken by about 165,000 people, mostly in the easternmost part of Latvia, known as **Latgale**. After the Polish–Swedish wars of the seventeenth century, the area inhabited by (old) Latvians was divided by the state border into Latgale, under the rule of the Polish-Lithuanian Commonwealth, and the rest of Latvia, under the rule of the Baltic Germans. This division lasted for several hundred years and permanently influenced the individual development of the Latgalian and Latvian languages.

Today, Latgalian is not used as an official language, but is protected as a literary language and as a historical variant of the Latvian language. Following independence from the Soviet Union, the Latgalian language is present in the media, music and partly in the educational system of Latgale. The city of **Rēzekne**, known as 'The Heart of Latgale', is home to the *Latgales Māra* sculpture. The inscription on the sculpture translates as 'United for Latvia', which symbolizes the unification of Latgale with the rest of Latvia, after 300 years of separation.

In the late nineteenth and early twentieth centuries, 20,000 to 50,000 Latgalians immigrated to Siberia. When the Soviet Union disintegrated in the early 1990s, many decided to stay in their homes in **Bobrovka** (known as 'Little Latvia of the Taiga'), **Achinsk**, **Barabinsk** and other Siberian settlements. All of them still jealously guard their folk costumes and traditional food, and celebrate old customs and holidays, while priests hold church services in the Latgalian language.

Latgales Māra monument, Rēzekne

This passage from the novella *The Little Prince* illustrates the differences between the Latgalian and Latvian languages:

Latgalian:
Ak, Mozais priņci! Moz pa mozam es suoču saprast tovu šaurū, biedeigū dzeivi. Cīš garu laiku tova vīneiguo prīca ir bejuse saulis rīta vāruošona. Itū seikumeņu es atkluoju catūrtuos dīnys reitā, kod tu maņ saceji: Maņ pateik, kai rīt saule.

Latvian:
Ai, mazo princi, tikai pamazām es sāku saprast tavu skumjo dzīvi! Ilgu laiku tev nebija citas izklaidēšanās kā vienīgi saulrietu skaistums. Šo jauno sīkumu uzzināju ceturtās dienas rītā, kad tu man teici: Man ļoti patīk saulrieti.

GERMANIC LANGUAGE ISLANDS

ENGLISH LANGUAGE ISLANDS

When, in the middle of the fifth century, the king of the **Celtic Britons** called on the Germanic tribes of **Angles**, **Jutes** and **Saxons** to help him fight the Picts and Scots, he probably had no idea that he was laying the groundwork for one of the most influential languages of modern civilization: **English**. It was the Angles – named after the Anglia peninsula on the northern coast of today's Germany – who gave their name to the English language and to **England**. Nearly five centuries later, the country was conquered by **Normans** from Northern France, who brought a new official language.

The result is a mixture of the **Germanic** languages of Angles, Jutes and Saxons, influenced by the languages of the Romance Normans and their allies, the Celtic Britons and the Germanic **Flemish**. The Normans themselves were a mixture of **Vikings**, **Franks** and **Gallo-Romance** people. This entire heritage created the English language, which today is the official language in almost seventy countries. It is probably the most widely spoken language ever, with about 400 million people speaking it as their first language, and yet English is still found in several locations around the world as an island surrounded by other languages.

The **Republic of Malta** is an island nation in the central part of the Mediterranean Sea. In terms of area, it is the tenth smallest country in the world, with 550,000 inhabitants on 316 square kilometres. **Maltese** is the official and national language. It is a direct descendant of **Sicilian Arabic**, which was the everyday language of the **Emirate of Sicily**, an Islamic state that spread on the islands of Sicily and Malta from the middle of the ninth to the end of the eleventh centuries. After the declaration of independence from the UK in 1964, Maltese and English were declared official languages, with a slight predominance of the Maltese language.

Official government documents are usually written in both English and Maltese; under Maltese law, in the event of any ambiguity in a document written in both languages, the Maltese text takes precedence. The majority of primary education is in English, while it is almost exclusively used in secondary and high schools. Maltese English has largely been influenced by the **Italian** language, primarily in the very noticeable accentuation of many words in the Italian way.

The UK's famous red telephone booths can still be seen in Malta

Gibraltar is a small, strategically important British Overseas Territory with high autonomy, located on one of the southernmost points of Europe. Attached to the Spanish mainland, the peninsula has belonged to the United Kingdom (UK) since 1713, and almost all Spanish governments have since demanded its return to Spanish sovereignty.

Gibraltar is a nation of just over 30,000 people, formed over the past 300 years as an amalgam of the British, Spanish from Andalusia, Genoans and other Italians, Portuguese, Maltese and other peoples. This has led to the creation of a specific language, known as **Llanito** or **Yanito**, which is basically **Andalusian Spanish** heavily influenced by English and **Ligurian** (**Genoese**). However, English is still the official language. This means that English is taught in all schools up to college age, and that English is the only official language of the Gibraltar authorities.

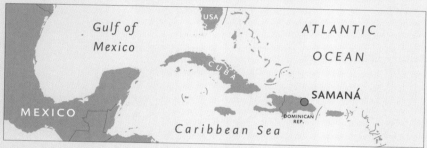

Samaná English is a dialect of American English spoken by a small number of elderly African American people on the **Samaná Peninsula** in the Spanish-speaking Dominican Republic. Speakers of this language are known as **Samaná Americans**, and their ancestors arrived on the peninsula in the first half of the nineteenth century from northeast United States at the invitation of the local authorities. The migration was not without its problems as there were significant cultural, linguistic and religious differences between the English-speaking Protestant newcomers and the Spanish-speaking Catholics who already lived there.

There were about 8,000 Samaná Americans in the mid-twentieth century, and although data suggests that up to 80 per cent of the current population of the province of Samaná is of African-American origin, it is increasingly difficult to find someone who is fluent in this language, even among the elderly inhabitants.

SCOTS

Scots is a **West Germanic** language, which is spoken today in parts of **Scotland** and **Ireland**. A thousand years ago, **Northern English** dialects were slowly beginning to displace **Scottish Gaelic** from the south of Scotland. Over the next few hundred years, these dialects became more and more widely accepted among the Scottish people, writers and royalty, and became known as the Scots language. However, the loss of Scottish sovereignty and the growing overall dominance of England led to an increasing use of English in Scotland as well, and the Scots language began to be associated with low education levels and poor knowledge of English.

Fortunately, such times are largely in the past, so today English and Scots are generally presented as sister languages, with Germanic languages in Scotland now seen as one linguistic continuum, with standard English at one end and Scots at the other. Scots is treated as an indigenous regional language, and a number of schools in Scotland have classes in this language.

In the middle of the sixteenth century, Scots speakers also inhabited the northern parts of Ireland, where their language became known as **Ulster Scots**. Since the Scots in Scotland are often referred to as **Lallans** (from the term 'lowland Scottish', as opposed to the **Celtic** 'highland Scottish'), the Irish variant is also known as **Ullans** ('Ulster' + 'Lallans'). Today, Ulster Scots is spoken in the northern part of **Northern Ireland**, and also in the Republic of Ireland, primarily in the eastern parts of **County Donegal**. It is estimated that there are between 35,000 and 100,000 Ulster Scots speakers on the island of Ireland.

The differences between Scots and English can be seen in this passage from *The Little Prince*:

Scots:
Ah! Prince-bairnie, that wes hou I cam tae unnerstaun, a bittie at a time, your dowie wee life. For mony a day ye hed naethin tae divert ye but the lown o the doungangs. I lairnt this new detail on the mornin o the fowert day, whan ye said tae me: I'm awfy fond o doungangs.

English:
Oh, little prince! Bit by bit I came to understand the secrets of your sad little life. For a long time you had found your only entertainment in the quiet pleasure of looking at the sunset. I learnt that new detail on the morning of the fourth day, when you said to me: I am very fond of sunsets.

Trilingual sign (English, Irish, Ulster Scots) in Northern Ireland

SWEDISH LANGUAGE ISLANDS

ELFDALIAN

Low population density and numerous isolated settlements throughout Scandinavia have led to the development of numerous dialects, where the problem of mutual understanding often exists. One of the most unusual dialects is the **Elfdalian** language (**älvdalska** in Swedish, **övdalsk** in Elfdalian). Yes, a growing number of linguists believe that this little-known and well-hidden dialect of **Swedish** is actually a separate language. Indeed, it is very difficult for the average Swede to understand a text written or spoken in Elfdalian.

It is probably the most archaic of all Scandinavian languages. Elfdalian is thought to have separated from **Old Norse**, the ancestor of all Scandinavian languages, as early as the end of the eighth century, around the same time Old Norse evolved into **Old West Norse**, **Old East Norse** and **Old Gutnish**.

Today, this language is spoken by just under half of the 7,000 inhabitants of the wooded, isolated town of **Älvdalen** in central Sweden. With the advent of radio and television, the number of speakers had begun to change drastically, as young people rapidly abandoned the use of their own language and switched to Swedish, the language of prosperous cities and the entertainment industry. The situation began to improve in the late 1980s, and the real breakthrough occurred in 2005, when the Elfdalian Language Council adopted a single standard spelling, which made it easier to print books in the language.

In 2015, the famous model Sofia Hellqvist married Prince Karl Filip, fourth in line to the Swedish throne. This was of great significance to the Elfdalian language, because Sofia's grandmother was from Älvdalen, and Sofia herself spent a large part of her younger years in the town. The first major benefit of this marriage was evident at the end of 2019, when Princess Sofia opened the Elfdalian kindergarten in Älvdalen, a crucial step in expanding the base of Elfdalian speakers.

Bilingual Swedish–Elfdalian signs in Älvdalen

Let us compare standard Swedish and Elfdalian with the help of *The Little Prince*:

Standard Swedish:
Min lille prins, så småningom kom jag underfund med hur dystert ditt liv var! Långa tider hade du ingen annan förströelse än underbara solnedgångar. Det förstod jag den fjärde dagen på morgonen, då du anförtrodde mig: Jag tycker så mycket om solnedgångar.

Elfdalian:
Undå för undå fuor ig föstå ur launggsamt du add eð, Lisslprinsn menn. Laindj i seð add it du noð eller uonå dig å eld kuogå å grannsuolniðgaunggą. Eð föstuoð ig um morgun fiuord da'n, mes du lit að mig: Ig tyttjer so mitjið um suolniðgaunggą.

GUTNISH

The island of **Gotland**, located in the Baltic Sea, is the largest Swedish island (actually an archipelago) with an area of almost 3,200 square kilometres and a population of just under 60,000. Approximately 2,000 people in the southern part of the main island and on a small neighbouring island in the north, **Fårö**, speak the **Gutnish** language.

The Gutnish language is related to Swedish, but the differences are so great that the average Swede simply will not understand much of what is said in Gutnish.

There are some linguists who believe that Gutnish is actually the last remnant of the former **East Germanic Gothic** language (the East Germanic language branch has died out), which has somehow survived for centuries after the extinction of the majority of Gothic languages, including the disappearance of the **Crimean Gothic** language at the turn of the nineteenth century.

GERMAN LANGUAGE ISLANDS IN EUROPE

German is a West Germanic language, which mainly spreads over a large part of Central Europe. It is the mother tongue of about 100 million people, and the most spoken language in the European Union. Given the number of speakers, it is not surprising that there are numerous dialects, as well as German language islands throughout Europe and the world!

GOTTSCHEERISH

The **Gottscheerish** (**Göttscheabarisch**) language is one of the oldest and (today) smallest German language islands. This island was initially located around the present-day town of **Kočevje** in the south of Slovenia. The first **Gottscheers** immigrated there in the middle of the fourteenth century from Tyrol and Carinthia (now Austrian federal states, then states within the **Holy Roman Empire**), and they maintained their language, customs and identity for 600 years.

After the Second World War, the new communist authorities of Yugoslavia expelled almost all Germans, including the Gottscheers. Today, most Gottscheers live in **New York**, United States. After 600 years of independent development, Gottscheerish and standard German are quite different, which is shown by a comparison of basic numbers in both languages:

	1	2	3	4	5	6	7	8	9	10
Gottscheerish	uains	tsboai	drai	viər	vemf	žekš	žĩbm	oxt	nain	tsēhŋ
German	eins	zwei	drei	vier	fünf	sechs	sieben	acht	neun	zehn

German and Gottscheerish inscription at the Chapel of the Holy Sepulchrei, Kočevje, Slovenia

DANUBE SWABIANS

The **Danube Swabians** are a large group of German speakers who inhabit or have inhabited an area around the Danube River. Migrations to this area were most intense during the seventeenth and eighteenth centuries, when the Austro-Hungarian authorities called on Germans from various parts of Central Europe to inhabit areas taken from the faltering Ottoman Empire. After the Second World War, most of the Danube Swabians were expelled from Yugoslavia, Romania and Hungary.

Banat Swabians are a group of the Danube Swabians inhabiting the area of **Banat,** currently divided between Romania and Serbia. Today, only a few thousand of them live in that area, while the largest number emigrated to the Austrian capital **Vienna** and also to America (**New York**, **Detroit** and **Cincinnati**). Probably the most famous Banat Swabian is *Tarzan*, that is, the famous actor and Olympic swimming champion Johnny Weissmuller, born János or Johann Weißmüller. Two settlements in Banat are listed as his possible birthplace: Freidorf (Szabadfalu or Szabadfalva in Hungarian), today part of Timişoara, Romania, where Johnny was baptized three days after his birth; or Párdány (present-day Međa, Serbia), which was given when the Weißmüller family immigrated to America.

Satu Mare Swabian or **Sathmar Swabian** (**Schwǫbisch** in the local dialect) is a dialect of Danubian German, spoken by German immigrants in the Romanian region of **Satu Mare**, near the border with Hungary and Ukraine. According to available data, only 200 people speak this dialect today.

CARPATHIAN GERMANS

Today, the term **Carpathian Germans** is usually applied to the population of German ethnic and linguistic origin in **Slovakia** and **Carpathian Ruthenia** in Ukraine. The Carpathian Germans inhabited this area mostly after the Mongol invasion in the middle of the thirteenth century. A large number of German settlements in and around the Carpathian Mountains were isolated from the majority of the German-speaking area, so over time, unusual and archaic local dialects developed, most of which are endangered today.

Zipser German (**Zipserisch** or **Zipserdeutsch** in German) is a dialect that originated among Germans living in the **Upper** and **Lower Zips** (**Spiš** in Slovak) areas of present-day Slovakia. In the southeast of Slovakia is the town of **Medzev** (**Metzenseifen** in German), which has been one of the centres of German culture and language for almost 700 years and where a separate German dialect, known as **Mantak**, developed. Rudolf Schuster, the second president (1999–2004) of independent Slovakia, is a Carpathian German from Medzev.

There were also many villages and towns inhabited by German speakers in Carpathian Ruthenia in Ukraine. **Nimetska Mokra** (**Deutsch Mokra** in German) is a place founded in 1775 by a group of about 100 lumberjacks and salt miners with their families from the Salzkammergut area (called Soizkaumaguad in the the local dialect) in today's Austrian federal state of Upper Austria. In this whole area today there are only 300 elderly people who, occasionally, use their old speech. It is interesting to note that they never learnt standard German, so they could only have a conversation with Austrians who know the old dialects of the Soizkaumaguad area.

Bilingual welcome sign in Ukraine

UPPER GERMAN DIALECTS IN ITALY

Upper German comprises the **Alemannic** and **Bavarian** dialect groups.

Walser German belongs to the group of Highest Alemannic dialects, spoken by about 4.5 million Swiss Germans and about 10,000 Walsers. It is a set of dialects spoken in parts of Liechtenstein, Switzerland – in the southern cantons of Valais, Ticino and Graubünden (Grisons) – and the Austrian province of Vorarlberg, as well as in the far north of Italy, around Monte Rosa mountain. The history of Walser German began in the fifth century, when the **Alemannic** (**Suebi**) tribal alliance began to occupy the valley of the upper course of the Rhône river, which roughly corresponds with the canton of Valais. During the twelfth and thirteenth centuries, their descendants began to spread to the surrounding parts of the Alps. Today, the Walser German dialect of the town of **Issime**, **Töitschu**, differs so much from the **Titsch** dialect spoken in the other two towns in Northern Italy – **Gressoney-St-Jean** and **Gressoney-La-Trinité** – that their speakers can hardly communicate.

Austro-Bavarian (more commonly known as **Bavarian**, or **Boarisch** in Bavarian) is a West Germanic language, spoken in most of Austria and the German federal state of Bavaria. In northern Italy, in the valleys of the Alps, there are several isolated villages in which archaic dialects of the Bavarian language are spoken.

Bersntol (**Valle del Fersina** in Italian), a valley in Northern Italy, is also known as **Valle dei Mòcheni**, 'the valley of Mocheno'. It got its alternative name from its inhabitants of German origin, known as **Mòcheno**, who speak an isolated dialect of Bavarian. The valley was settled in the fourteenth century, and today the **Mòcheno** language has about 1,600 speakers. They got their unusual name from their Italian neighbours, due to the frequent use of the verb *mochen* ('to work'). It is the majority language in three municipalities (Fierozzo/Vlarotz, Frassilongo/Garait, Palù del Fersina/Palai En Bersntol). Mòcheno is protected by the laws of the Autonomous Province of Trento, and school classes are held in that language, while traffic signs are bilingual.

Another Germanic language is spoken, though less and less, south of the Bersntol valley. This language is known as **Cimbrian** and centuries of isolation have made it almost completely incomprehensible to speakers of standard German, and even to most speakers of Bavarian. Approximately 2,200 speakers of Cimbrian inhabit a handful of villages and towns: **Roana/Robàan, Giazza/Ljetzan** and **Luserna/Lusérn**.

The towns of **Sauris** (**Zahre** in German; 420 inhabitants) and **Sappada** (**Plodn** in Sappadino; 1,300 inhabitants) are home to two related Bavarian dialects: **Saurano**, which contains numerous outdated features of **Tyrolean** dialects, and **Sappadino** (**Plodarsich**).

A large number of older residents of the village of **Timau** (**Tischlbong** in the local dialect) still use **Tischlbongarisch**, a dialect derived from **Carinthian** dialects with a large influence of Romance languages. Today, children learn Tischlbongarisch in kindergartens and primary schools.

The difference between standard German, Walser German and the Cimbrian language can also be seen by comparing the same passage from *The Little Prince*:

Standard German:
Ach, kleiner Prinz, so nach und nach habe ich dein kleines schwermütiges Leben verstanden. Lange Zeit hast du, um dich zu zerstreuen, nichts anderes gehabt als die Lieblichkeit der Sonnenuntergänge. Das erfuhr ich am Morgen des vierten Tages, als du mir sagtest: Ich liebe die Sonnenuntergänge sehr.

Walser German:
Ach, chliine Prinz! So naat zu naat hani dis chlii, schwärmiätigs Läbu verschtandu. Lang hesch als Ablänkig nur d'Freid ane Sunnuunergäng ka. Das hani ersch am Morgu vam viärtu Tag erfaaru, wa du z'miär gseit hesch: Ich ha gäru Sunnuunnergäng.

Cimbrian:
Oh khlumma printz, i hån vorstånt laise laise doi khlumma trauregez lem. Vor långa zait hasto nèt gehatt åndarst baz daz süaz vodar sunn boda oinegeat. Eppaz mearar hånne darvert in viarte tage, mòrgas, baldomar hast khött: 'Z gevalltmar asó vil seng gian oine di sunn.

GERMAN LANGUAGE ISLANDS IN NORTH AMERICA

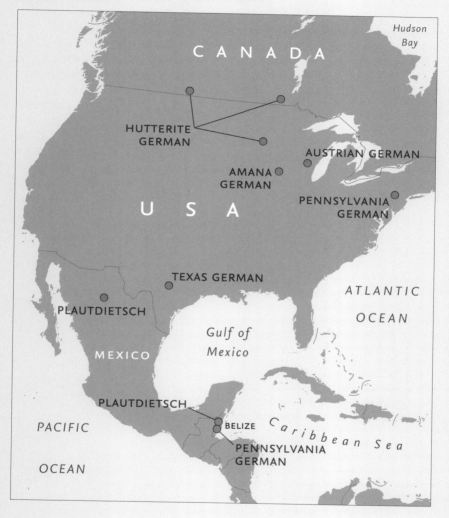

Hudson Bay

CANADA

HUTTERITE GERMAN

AUSTRIAN GERMAN

AMANA GERMAN

U S A

PENNSYLVANIA GERMAN

TEXAS GERMAN

ATLANTIC OCEAN

PLAUTDIETSCH

Gulf of Mexico

MEXICO

PLAUTDIETSCH

PACIFIC

BELIZE

Caribbean Sea

PENNSYLVANIA GERMAN

OCEAN

AMANA COLONIES

The desire to freely profess one's religion has led to numerous religious groups moving to distant parts of the world, hoping to find their peace. Thus, in the middle of the nineteenth century, after encountering numerous problems with the official Lutheran Church and the German state, a group of Lutheran believers known as the **Pietists** decided to go and freely express their religious views on the other side of the Atlantic Ocean. After founding several colonies in the state of New York, these German migrants decided to find a quieter location, and moved in groups to the state of Iowa, where they founded the **Amana Colonies**. Amana consists of seven villages, each of which has its own church, school, shop, wine cellar, dairy, and also a fire brigade.

Today, there are several hundred people in the Amana Colonies who speak **Amana German** (**Kolonie-Deutsch**), and thanks to the regular use of the language, it is believed that it is not in danger of extinction.

AUSTRIAN AMERICANS

The first **Austrian** migrants emigrated from Salzburg in 1734 and built their settlement in the New World – the town of **Ebenezer**, in Georgia, on the border with South Carolina.

Today, there are only two settlements in the United States where more than 10 per cent of Americans of Austrian descent live: **Waterville** in Wisconsin and **Coplay** in Pennsylvania. Among the most famous Austrian-Americans are Arnold Schwarzenegger, a famous actor, bodybuilder and former governor of California, and actors Woody Allen (born Allan Stewart Konigsberg) and Fred Astaire (born Frederick Austerlitz), whose father was from the Austrian city of Linz. If we expand our view to the whole of North America, we can see another interesting Austrian: the only emperor of the Second Mexican Empire was Maximilian I (reigned: 1864–1867), the younger brother of Emperor Franz Joseph I of Austria.

TEXAS GERMANS

Texas German is spoken by a (small) group of descendants of German migrants, primarily from the central parts of Germany. They inhabited Texas in the middle of the nineteenth century, when they founded a dozen towns in central and southern Texas. It is assumed that today there is a negligibly small number of young people who know the Texas version of the German language, while there are several thousand older speakers.

The town of **Fredericksburg** (**Friedrichsburg** in German; 9,000 inhabitants) is home to the largest number of people of German descent, who often call their town **Fritztown**. Approximately 40 per cent of Fredericksburg residents are of German descent, and 12 per cent use Texas German daily.

GERMAN MEXICANS

The first German emigrants settled in Mexico in the middle of the nineteenth century. Probably the most famous member of the **German Mexicans** is the acclaimed painter Frida Kahlo, whose father was born in Germany.

Another group of German speakers (or at least one of its specific dialects) inhabits Mexico in large numbers. There are more than 110,000 German Mexican **Mennonites** who use the **Plautdietsch** language almost exclusively, a language that originated as a mixture of **Low German** and **Dutch**. The largest number of Mennonites, about 90,000 of them, settled in the northern Mexican federal state of Chihuahua. The highest concentration of Mennonites is around the city of **Cuauhtémoc**, where the three official languages are Spanish, English and Plautdietsch.

Several groups of Mennonites from Mexico established their colonies in neighbouring Belize. The most well-known of these colonies is **Spanish Lookout**, a town with about 2,500 inhabitants, almost all of whom speak Plautdietsch.

HUTTERITES

The **Hutterites** are another Protestant community – although they consider their beliefs to be a separate branch of Christianity – originating in sixteenth-century Europe, that has found its own peace in the prairies of Canada and the United States. Although at one point in its history its numbers fell to only 400, this religious and linguistic group today has 45,000 members (three-quarters in Canada, one-quarter in the United States). Children in these colonies first learn **Hutterite German**, and only then English, while schooling according to the Hutterite programme is done in schools within their territory.

Hutterite German is a language originally based on Bavarian dialects from Tyrol (the founder of this religious group was Jacob Hutter from today's South Tyrol in Italy). Over time, increasing numbers of Hutterites came from Carinthia, so the language progressively absorbed characteristics of Carinthian dialects of the German language. Today, Hutterite German is considered a mixture of the two initial dialects, with a number of words borrowed from Russian and English.

Hutterite women in traditional clothing, Greenwood Hutterite Colony, South Dakota

PENNSYLVANIA GERMAN

Pennsylvania German or **Pennsylvania Dutch** (**Pennsilfaanisch-Deitsch**) is a variant of the German language that is mostly used today by certain conservative groups of **Amish** and Mennonites in a number of American states. The total number of speakers is estimated at around 300,000, and the highest concentration is in **Pennsylvania**, where approximately a third of the population is of German ethnic origin. A large number of speakers can also be found in **Ohio**, **Indiana**, **Wisconsin** and **Iowa**. Fun fact: the name 'Dutch' comes from the word *Deitsch*, which in the dialects of the ancestors of today's speakers of Pennsylvania German means *Deutsch* ('German').

Interestingly, Pennsylvania German has expanded south since the early 1970s, when a new Mennonite colony, **Upper Barton Creek**, was founded in Belize. The colony was established so that its members (currently 400) could live without the use of modern aids (no electricity or cars are used, and the fields are cultivated by hand and with the help of horses). Education is provided in primary schools within the colony; higher levels of education are not allowed.

GERMAN LANGUAGE ISLANDS IN SOUTH AMERICA

Caribbean Sea

COLONIA
TOVAR GERMAN

VENEZUELA

ATLANTIC OCEAN

COLOMBIA

B R A Z I L

BOLIVIA
PLAUTDIETSCH

PARAGUAY

HUNSRIK

PACIFIC OCEAN

ARGENTINA

ATLANTIC OCEAN

COLONIA TOVAR GERMAN

In the middle of the nineteenth century, a group of 400 people from the German Grand Duchy of Baden (southwestern part of present-day Germany) set out on a journey across the Atlantic Ocean all the way to Venezuela. There, at 2,200 metres above sea level, they built their settlement, which they named **Colonia Tovar**. By the start of the Second World War, the settlement had fully earnt its nickname, *Germany of the Caribbean* – the church and houses were built in the South German style, the inhabitants spoke their Alemannic dialect, and the isolation of the settlement allowed a kind of cultural autonomy for Colonia Tovar. Unfortunately, the war led to a complete ban on the use of the language, and the post-war period brought the construction of a quality road, which facilitated the rapid infux of a large number of Spanish speakers. Today, only 1,500 elderly Colonia Tovar residents speak **Alemán Coloniero**, as their German dialect is called in Spanish.

Iglesia San Martín de Tours, Aragua, Venezuela

HUNSRIK

Brazil's three southernmost states, **Rio Grande do Sul**, **Santa Catarina** and **Paraná**, are home to another group of German speakers. In this case it is a language called **Hunsrik** or **Riograndenser Hunsrückisch**. This South American speech was brought in the middle of the nineteenth century by immigrants from Hunsrück, a German region along the border with Luxembourg and France. In Brazil, Plautdietsch, Portuguese, and also indigenous languages (**Guaraní, Kaingang**) and immigrant languages (**Venetian**, Italian) had a great influence on the formation of Hunsrik.

Today, Hunsrik is a co-official language in several Brazilian municipalities and is also used in smaller border areas of Argentina and Paraguay.

The Little Prince has also been translated into Hunsrik:

Ah!, kleene prins, soo wii ich aankefang hon se ferxteen, noo un noo, ti kehëmnis fon tayn traurich leeweche. Iwich en lang tsayt hast tuu khee aner ferkniichung kehat als ti siisichkheet fom unerkang fon te sun. Tee noye tetayl hon ich kelërnt wii tuu mich saast, moynts, am fierte taach: Ich hon te sune unerkang aarich kërn.

The most German city in Brazil is located in the state of Santa Catarina. This flattering title is proudly carried by the city of **Pomerode**, where 90 per cent of the 35,000 inhabitants speak some of the German dialects. Nearby is **Blumenau** (360,000 inhabitants), a city founded in the nineteenth century by a German chemist and pharmacist of the same name. German heritage is widely evident, from buildings and houses built in typical German style to the eighteen-day festival of German tradition and entertainment, the *Oktoberfest of Blumenau*.

Oktoberfest of Blumenau, Brazil

PLAUTDIETSCH

The **Mennonites** in Bolivia came to the country seeking freedom both for their way of life and for practising their religious beliefs as they had in the Old World. Smaller Mennonite groups occupied sparsely populated areas of Bolivia between the two world wars, but the majority of new settlers arrived in the 1960s and 1970s from Mexico, Paraguay and Canada. This ethno-religious group primarily uses the **Plautdietsch** language, just like most of their religious counterparts across the Americas. Mennonites in Bolivia are among the most conservative members of their religious community.

The Bolivian authorities guaranteed the Mennonites complete religious freedom, as well as the right to private schools and exemption from military service. All of these rights, along with a strong work ethic, led the Mennonite colonies to flourish in Bolivia. Today, approximately 50,000 Mennonites live in several dozen colonies, surrounded by fertile fields and orchards. With 5,000 members, the largest colony is the **Riva Palacios Colony**, which is located 60 kilometres south of the city of Santa Cruz. Many Mennonite villages have their own private schools. Interestingly, although most members of the colonies speak Plautdietsch, church sermons are usually held in standard German, which is not known to many Mennonites.

GERMAN LANGUAGE ISLANDS IN OTHER PARTS OF THE WORLD

GERMANS IN RUSSIA

The historical ties between the Russians and Germans are intertwined, both in war and in peace. After the Second World War, most Germans were expelled from the Soviet Union, although the ancestors of many of them had lived on Russian soil for hundreds of years, often at the invitation of Russian emperors and empresses.

Today, there are two districts in Russia, near the city of Omsk, that are inhabited by a large number of Germans. Both districts are located in southwestern Siberia, close to the border with Kazakhstan. The **German National District** has an area of 1,450 square kilometres and a total population of 17,700, of which 4,700 are German. The administrative centre of the district is Gal'bshtadt (Halbstadt in German). After the collapse of the Soviet Union, Germany began to give financial support to its compatriots in Asia, building roads, new residential buildings, manufacturing facilities, schools and hospitals. Unfortunately, that was not enough to prevent many Germans from this district returning to Germany. Not far from the German National District is **Asovo German National District**, with the town of Asovo (Asowo in German) as its centre. There are 4,500 Germans living in the district out of a total population of 23,000. Here, also, many took the opportunity to emigrate to Germany, and among those that have remained, a large number no longer speak German.

In the Omsk region, near the town of **Isil'kul'**, there are a few villages inhabited by Mennonites, where Plautdietsch is still spoken.

GERMANS IN NEW ZEALAND AND NEW GUINEA

The village of **Puhoi** is located 50 kilometres north of Auckland, New Zealand. The first European settlers in Puhoi and the neighbouring **Ōhaupō** were German-speaking emigrants from the town of Stod (Staab in German) in Bohemia, then part of the Austro-Hungarian Empire. After the outbreak of the First World War and the very great animosity that the inhabitants of New Zealand felt towards the Germans, the inhabitants of Puhoi slowly began to present their settlement as a *Bohemian Settlement* according to their regional, rather than ethnic, origin.

The library of Puhoi Town is one of the smallest in New Zealand

Their descendants have preserved numerous customs, folk costumes and music, but also their unusual speech – **Puhoi Egerländer** dialect, which is based on the Bavarian dialects of today's far west of Czechia (Czech Republic). Unfortunately, it is believed that there are only a few people today with a more-or-less complete knowledge of this New Zealand German dialect, so there are fewer and fewer people who can be greeted with *Wöi göiht's?* ('How are you?') and have their good health wished for with *Bleib g'sund!* ('Stay well!'/'Goodbye!').

At the beginning of the twentieth century, the northern part of Papua New Guinea was a German colony called **German New Guinea**. There was a Catholic school in the capital – **Kokopo** (**Herbertshöhe** in German) – of the province of East New Britain on the island of New Britain, attended by children from mixed families. In this school, the children learnt standard German, but at the same time gradually created their own language, a mixture of German and the local languages, mainly Tok Pisin. The customs of that time required that people of mixed origin usually marry within their own community, so these children did the same when they grew up, which helped keep their language, **Unserdeutsch** ('our German'), active to this day. After the independence of Papua New Guinea in 1975, almost all speakers of 'our German' moved to Australia. Today there are about 100 speakers in Australia, mostly in **Queensland**, and a dozen speakers remaining on the island of New Britain.

GERMANS IN NAMIBIA AND SOUTH AFRICA

Throughout the nineteenth century, Germany was the colonial power in Namibia, then known as **German South West Africa**, so it is not surprising that the influence of its rule is still noticeable in this country. Today, about 30,000 people of German origin live in Namibia, which represents a third of all Whites in this country.

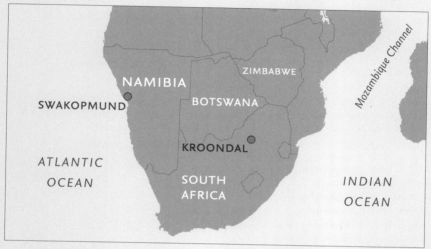

According to the latest statistics, in the coastal town of **Swakopmund**, 5 per cent of the population speaks German, which is probably the highest percentage of anywhere in this region. Across Namibia, German is used in about 4,300 households, which represent 1 per cent of the total number of households. Namibia's oldest daily newspaper, the *Allgemeine Zeitung* ('General Newspaper'), was founded in 1916 and is now the only German-language daily newspaper in Africa and the most widely read newspaper in Namibia.

German is spoken by less than 0.1 per cent of the population of South Africa, or 12,000 people. One place with a significant German minority is **Kroondal**, a village in North West Province, where a large percentage of the 3,500 inhabitants speaks German.

AND A FEW MORE GERMANIC LANGUAGE ISLANDS...

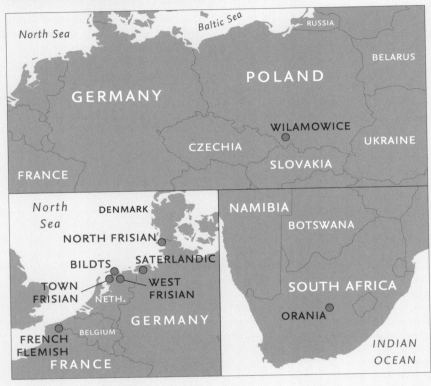

WYMYSORYS, POLAND

The town of **Wilamowice** is located in the south of Poland and has about 3,000 inhabitants. Most of them speak Polish, but a small contingent (fewer than 100) speaks an unusual (micro) language, which they call **Wymysiöeryś** (**Wymysorys** or **Vilamovian** in English). This is a Germanic language, which officially belongs to the German dialects. However, most Vilamovians have never regarded themselves as German, which is what saved them from being expelled from Poland after the Second World War.

In a way, the history of the Vilamovians begins in 1241, when the unstoppable Mongols stormed through Europe, devastating towns and villages, killing the local populations and destroying the economies of the countries they raided. Poland was one of those countries, so the rulers of that time invited people from the west of Europe to come, settle the abandoned villages and restart agriculture and trade. According to Vilamovian folklore, which is supported to some extent by research, their ancestors immigrated to Poland from various places: from Flanders, the northern part of today's Belgium; from Frisia, which includes the northern parts of the Netherlands and Germany, all the way to Denmark; and from Scotland. The result of mixing the settlers' languages, with the additional influence of the local Polish language and German dialects, is the specific and unique Wymysorys language.

Bilingual Polish/Wymysorys welcome sign in Wilamowice, Poland

FRISIAN LANGUAGES

Anglo-Frisian languages represent a group of West Germanic languages spoken today in the United Kingdom and Ireland (English and Scots), as well as in the Netherlands and Germany (**Frisian** languages).

Frisian languages are spoken by half a million people on the southern shores of the North Sea in the Netherlands and Germany; they are divided into three mutually unintelligible languages:

- The **West Frisian** language (**Frysk**; 400,000 speakers) is the official language of the Dutch province of **Friesland**.

- The **North Frisian** language (**Nordfriisk**) is used by fewer than 10,000 people in the northernmost part of Germany, along the border with Denmark. It consists of a dozen dialects, one of which is **Heligolandic** (**Halunder** in the dialect), spoken by a third of the 1,500 inhabitants of the German island of **Heligoland** in the North Sea.

- The most interesting language is **Saterland Frisian** or **Saterlandic** (**Seeltersk**), the last living dialect of the **East Frisian** language, which is spoken today by 2,250 inhabitants of several villages in the municipality of **Saterland** (10,000 inhabitants in total) in northern Germany. Most speakers belong to the older generation, so it can be said that the Saterlandic language belongs to the endangered languages. However, the latest information shows a slight increase in the use of the mother tongue among younger people, and it is becoming increasingly common for parents to teach their young children Saterlandic.

In the Dutch province of **Friesland** (**Fryslân** in West Frisian), 45,000 people today speak **Town Frisian** (**Stadsfries** in Dutch) and 5,000 people speak **Bildts**. These are both hybrids of Dutch and Frisian.

AFRIKAANS LANGUAGE ISLANDS

The Dutch language reached South Africa via numerous emigrants from the Netherlands. Over time, helped by the great distance from the motherland and the influence of the surrounding languages, the language of Dutch immigrants changed so much that it became a new language, with its own vocabulary, spelling and grammar rules, along with a new name – **Afrikaans**, which means 'African' in Dutch. Afrikaans is considered the daughter of the Dutch language and one of the youngest languages in the world.

During the apartheid period in South Africa, Afrikaans was the main language of the White ruling class. Following the end of racial division in 1994, Afrikaans became one of only eleven (!) official languages. To some Afrikaners, it seemed as though their culture, religion and, above all, their language was in danger. This is why a group of Afrikaners bought a piece of land (complete with an abandoned temporary workers' settlement) almost in the centre of South Africa, where they founded a town named **Orania**. The process of forming the town was long and not at all easy, but the result today is a relatively successful and prosperous town, with a high quality of life and a strong economy. Orania has its own currency (Ora, from the Latin *aurum*, meaning 'gold'), flag, schools, banks, radio station and hospital. The only language spoken by the 1,800 inhabitants in Orania is Afrikaans, and it is used in all classes in primary and secondary schools (English is also taught as a second language).

Orania, South Africa

FRENCH FLEMISH

The **Flemish** language is a continuum of dialects spoken in the northern and western parts of Belgium, as well as in small areas in the south of the Netherlands, and in the north of France. The Flemish language spoken in the north of France is called **French Flemish** (**Fransch vlaemsch**). It used to be the dominant language in this corner of France, but for several decades the number of speakers has been declining rapidly, so that today there is no settlement in which only Flemish is spoken – and a hundred years ago, such settlements were the most numerous. Today, French Flemish is spoken by approximately 10,000 people, mostly in the predominantly agricultural area of **Houtland** (Flemish for 'woodland').

SIMILARITIES AND DIFFERENCES IN GERMANIC LANGUAGE ISLANDS

These translations of *The Little Prince* illustrate the similarities and differences between Wymysorys, the Frisian languages, Flemish, Afrikaans and Dutch:

Wymysorys:
Ju, kliner fjyśt! Śtyklawåjz kom yh uf dåj klin, medytjynfuł ława. Łangy cåjt ferbłyn nok dy myłda zunaundergeng. Yhy kom uf dos à dryta tag s'mügjys, wy dy mer höst gyziöet: Yh łiw zunaundergeng.

West Frisian:
Och, lytse prins, sa stadichoan begûn ik wat sicht op dyn lytse mankelike libben te krijen. Do hiest skoftenlang gjin oare ferdivedaasje as de wille oan it ûndergean fan de sinne. Dat hearde ik de moarns fan de fjirde dei doe'tst tsjin my seidest: Ik mei graach oer it ûndergean fan de sinne.

North Frisian (island of Sylt dialect):
Aach litj Prins, me di Tir haa ik dach din litj swaar Leewent forstön. En lung Tir heest dü, bluat om wat tö dön, nönt üđers her üs di dailk Önergang fan di Sen tötölukin. Dit fing ik miarens, di fjaart Dai tö weeten, üs dü mi sairst: Ik mai en Senönergang sa hol liir.

Saterland Frisian:

Oach, litje Prins, so mäd de Tied hääbe iek dien litje sweermoudige Lieuwend begriepen. Man een loange Tied hääst du niks uurs häiwed, as dät ju Sunne sinnich unnergeen, wan du die moal ferpuustje wüült. Dät wude iek wies an dän Mäiden fon dän fjoode Dai, as du tou mie kweeden hääst: Iek mai so aiske jädden sjo, wan smoals ju Sunne unnergungt.

Flemish:

Oh mijn Klein Prinske, melankoniek boaske, zuu verstoa kik, beetse baa beetse eu leeve. G' hêt langen taad als aflaadijnge nie anders g'had dan het rustgeevende gevoel van de zonsondergange. 'k Hê da nieuw détail ontdekt, de vierden dag, tsmorges, oas ge maa gezaad hêt: Ik zie geere de zonsondergange.

Afrikaans:

A, klein prinsie, so het ek stadigaan iets van jou lewetjie en sy hartseer begin verstaan. 'n baie lang tyd was die lieflikheid van die sonsondergang vir jou die enigste plesier op jou planeet - dit het ek agtergekom toe jy op die oggend van die vierde dag vir my sê: Ek hou baie van sonsondergange.

Dutch:

Ach, kleine prins, zo heb ik langzamerhand je droefgeestige leventje leren begrijpen. Lange tijd had je geen andere afleiding dan het ondergaan van de zon. Dat hoorde ik de vierde dag, toen je zei: Ik hou erg van zonsondergangen.

ROMANCE LANGUAGE ISLANDS

Romance languages represent a large language group, formed in the period from the third to the eighth centuries and based on spoken **Latin**, which over time spread to Western, Southern and Southeastern Europe, as well as to South and North America and Africa. Today, over 900 million people around the world speak Romance languages. The most widely spoken is Spanish, with 490 million speakers, followed by Portuguese with 250 million, and **French** with almost 80 million. Italian is considered to be the closest to classical Latin, with French having undergone the greatest amount of change. Nevertheless, all Romance languages today are closer to each other than any of them are to Latin. The rough division of the Romance languages looks like this:

- **Eastern Romance** languages (spoken in the Balkan Peninsula and southern Italy)

- **Central Romance** or **Italo-Dalmatian** languages (spoken in central and southern Italy, Sicily and parts of Sardinia)

- **Western Romance** languages (roughly speaking, languages spoken in France, Spain, Italy, Portugal and their former and present colonies)

- **Sardinian** language, as a separate branch of Romance languages

ROMANCE LANGUAGE ISLANDS ON THE BALKAN PENINSULA

Let's start by looking at the language islands of the Eastern Romance languages, which today are divided into two subgroups:

- **Castelmezzano** dialect from southern Italy.

- **Balkano-Romanian** languages consist of the **Romanian** language along with the **Vlach** language in Serbia, the **Aromanian** language, **Megleno-Romanian** and **Istro-Romanian**.

CASTELMEZZANO, ITALY

In the south of the Apennine Peninsula, between the toes and the heel of the Italian 'boot', there is an Eastern Romance speech – the only one outside the Balkan Peninsula – the **Castelmezzano** dialect. This dialect is spoken in the town of the same name and its surroundings. The town of Castelmezzano (Castrëmënzànë in Castelmezzano dialect) is renowned for its beauty and belongs to an association named *I Borghi più belli d'Italia* in Italian ('Italy's most beautiful villages').

Night view of Castelmezzano after a snowfall

AROMANIAN

The **Aromanian** language (**armãneashce** in Aromanian) originated from the mixing of the vernacular Latin with the languages of the **Paleo-Balkan** peoples (namely **Thracian** and **Illyrian**) most likely after they became Romanized.

Aromanians call themselves **Rrãmãnji** or **Armãni**, while their neighbours usually call them **Vlachs** or **Cincars** (**Tsintsars**). The town of **Kruševo** (**Crushuva** in Aromanian, **Krusheva** in Albanian) in North Macedonia is a trilingual city and the only city in the world where Aromanian is one of the official languages, the other two being Macedonian and Albanian. The city therefore has three official names. Of the 5,500 inhabitants of Kruševo, 20 per cent are Aromanian. State radio and television regularly broadcast in Aromanian, and some school lessons are conducted in this language.

The village of **Metsovo** (**Aminciu** in Aromanian; 6,500 inhabitants) is the main centre of Aromanian culture not only in Greece, but also in the entire Balkan Peninsula. Another important Aromanian centre in Greece is the village of **Samarina**, located on the slopes of the Pindus Mountains. With an altitude ranging between 1,380 and 1,515 metres, the village is one of the highest populated places on the Balkan Peninsula.

Grabovë e Sipërme (**Grabuva** in Aromanian) is another Aromanian village, located in the southeastern part of Albania. Cyril of Bulgaria, the first Patriarch of the restored Bulgarian Patriarchate (1953–1971), and Andrei Șaguna, Metropolitan bishop of the Romanian Orthodox Church in Transylvania in the nineteenth century, were both from here.

The **Megleno-Romanian** language (**Vlŭheşte**) is either a Romance language or a transitional form between Romanian and Aromanian. It is spoken today by about 5,000 people in a small area on the border between Greece and Northern Macedonia, and by a few thousand people in Romania.

A few sentences from *The Little Prince* can show us what Aromanian looks like:

Ah! Amirãrush njic, duchii niheam cãti niheam njica a ta banã melancolicã. Multu chiro nu avushi altã harauã cã mashi ascãpitata a soarlui. Ãnvitsai aestã, patra dzuã, tahina, cãndu-nj dzãseshi: Mi ariseashti multu ascãpitata a soarlui.

ISTRO-ROMANIAN, CROATIA

One of the smallest ethnic groups in the world, the **Istro-Romanians** (**rumeri** or **rumâri** in Istro-Romanian) are one of the Eastern Romance peoples, who have inhabited the Istrian Peninsula in the northern Adriatic for hundreds of years, not far from the mountain range of the magnificent Alps.

Today, the Istro-Romanians are divided into two groups: north of the Učka mountains in the village of **Žejane** (**Jeiăn** in Istro-Romanian), and south of this mountain range in the village of **Šušnjevica**. The speech of the village of Žejane is the best preserved, both in terms of the number of speakers and the fact that it is in everyday use. Istro-Romanians are the only Balkan-Romanian people whose members are of the Catholic faith, which could account for a faster assimilation, since all priests hold their sermons exclusively in the Croatian language.

Only a few kilometres from the Adriatic coast of Istria and a few dozen kilometres from the Učka mountains and the area where Istro-Romanian is still spoken, is the village of **Bale** (**Vale**), where approximately 400 inhabitants speak a language known as **Istriot**. This is a Romance language, probably most closely related to Ladin and other languages from the Rhaeto-Romance group; it is not related to Istro-Romanian. A small number of Istriot speakers migrated after the Second World War to Sardinia, around the town of **Fertilia**.

Traditional carnival costume in Žejane (Jeiăn), Croatia

ROMANCE LANGUAGE ISLANDS IN SARDINIA

ALGHERESE

The **Algherese** (**alguerés**) language, a variant of the **Old Catalan** language, is spoken in the city of **Alghero** (**L'Alguer** in Algherese; 45,000 inhabitants) on the northwest coast of Sardinia.

During the fourteenth century, the **Crown of Aragon** countries covered a large part of the western Mediterranean. After an unsuccessful revolt at the end of the century, the former population of the city of Alghero was displaced, and a large number of Catalans were brought in their place. Despite strong Italianization, today one fifth of the population of the city and its immediate surroundings consider Algherese to be their mother tongue. Since the end of the twentieth century, Algherese has been co-official and protected by the Italian state; its use in literature and music is rather developed, and many books are being translated, including *The Little Prince*:

> Algherese:
> *Ah! Petit príncip, j he comprès, a poc a poc, la tua petita vida malenconiosa. Per tant temps, tu no has tengut altra distracció, que la dolçor de les colgades del sol. Ha sabut aqueix particular nou, lo quart dia, al maití, quan m'havies dit: M'agraden tant les colgades del sol.*

Catalan:

Ah!, petit príncep, d'aquesta manera, i a poc a poc, vaig anar entenent la teva petita vida malenconiosa. Durant molt de temps, l'única distracció que havies tingut havia estat la dolçor de les postes de sol. Vaig saber aquest altre detall el matí del quart dia, quan em vas dir: M'agraden molt les postes de sol.

Algherese is not considered a corrupt variant of the Catalan language, but a sister language, which developed under different circumstances from Old Catalan in Catalonia and Valencia.

TABARCHINO

The Ligurian or Genoese language is a **Gallo-Italic** language, spoken in the vicinity of Genoa and Monaco.

Off the southwest coast of Sardinia there are two small towns – **Carloforte** on San Pietro Island and **Calasetta** on Sant'Antioco Island. The Ligurian dialect of these two towns is known as **Tabarchino**. The history of the Ligurian presence in the south of Sardinia begins in the middle of the sixteenth century, when thirty families of coral fishers left the town of Pegli near Genoa and settled on the island of Tabarka off the northern coast of Tunisia. About two centuries later, sponges became increasingly difficult to find, so the settlers from Genoa decided to return to the land of their ancestors. However, they learnt that in the south of Sardinia, next to the uninhabited island of San Pietro, were large stocks of sponges, so they asked the King of Sardinia, Charles Emmanuel III, for permission to build a town on the island – later named Carloforte in gratitude to the King – for themselves. Their request was granted, just as it was for another group of similar origin, who built their settlement, Calasetta, on neighbouring Sant'Antioco Island.

The inhabitants of Carloforte (U Pàize in Ligurian, 'the town'; 6,200 inhabitants) today speak a rather modern Ligurian language with very few archaisms, similar to that used in Genoa. On the other hand, in Calasetta (Câdesédda in Ligurian), a much more archaic language is spoken, more similar to the language spoken on the island of Tabarka and in Genoa in the sixteenth century.

The Little Prince can illustrate the differences between the Ligurian (Genoese) and Tabarchino languages:

Ligurian:
Ah! Prinçipìn, ò compréizo, ciancianìn, coscì, a teu vitta piciña e malincònica de figeu solo. O l'ëa de pe coscì che pe a teu distraçión ti no avéivi avùo nintätro che o doçe di tramonti. Ò capïo sta nœvitœ o quarto giorno, de matìn, quande ti m'œ dïto: Me piaxan tanto i tramonti.

Tabarchino:
Oh prìncipe picin, à pócu à pócu ho acapìu a tó piciña e triste vitta. Pe tantu tempu ti nu t'è avüu otru che a beléssa di tramunti. Ho acapìu sti nöi aspetti de ti â matin du quòrtu giurnu, quande ti m'è ditu: Végnu mattu pai tramunti.

A typical street in the village of Carloforte

ROMANCE LANGUAGE ISLANDS ON THE IBERIAN PENINSULA

The Iberian Peninsula and its 55 million inhabitants are divided between the majority Romance nations of Spain, Portugal, Andorra, (southern) France and the British Overseas Territory of Gibraltar, in which the majority of the population is also of Romance origin. Although at first glance it sounds as though the Iberian Peninsula is linguistically compact and homogeneous, several Romance linguistic islands still stand out.

MIRANDESE

Lhéngua mirandesa is a dialect of the extreme northeast of Portugal, a dialect or variant of the **Astur-Leonese** language spoken in neighbouring Spain. Mirandese is the mother tongue of about 5,000 people, while another 10,000 speak it occasionally. This speech arose as a consequence of the isolation of a smaller group of speakers of the Astur-Leonese language, which led to a difference between written and spoken language compared to that in Spain, including a larger number of archaisms and new grammatical and spelling features.

In 1998, the Portuguese Parliament granted the Mirandese language official status in the historic area of **Terra de Miranda** (an area of about 500 square kilometres on the border with Spain), which brought about some positive changes towards the preservation of the language. The problem is that young people often do not want to learn this language, because they think that they will not benefit from it in the future.

MINDERICO

Minderico (**Piação do Ninhou** in Minderico: 'the language of Minde') is a secret language or *sociolect* invented by workers in the textile industry and trade. This unusual speech originated in the eighteenth century in the town of **Minde** (**Ninhou** in Minderico), after which it was named. Today, approximately 500 people today use Minderico, and efforts are being made to collect linguistic material which should help to strengthen the language. Due to the small number of speakers of this language and the fact that almost all of these people knew each other, it was not unusual to use the name or nickname of a Minderico speaker to express his or her characteristic feature in a conversation (for example, the name of a tall person would be used to replace the adjective 'tall').

Minderico has undergone an interesting evolution, developing from the secret speech of a closed social group to the language known to many people in the Portuguese city of Minde and its surroundings.

ARAGONESE

Aragonese is a Western Romance language, spoken today in the northern areas of the **Autonomous Community of Aragon,** on the slopes and in the valleys of the Pyrenees. The number of speakers is in decline, with current numbers estimated at about 10,000, plus a further 20,000 with basic knowledge of the language. The common name for Aragonese is **fabla** ('talk'), although most speakers call it by the name of their dialect, for example **cheso** in Valle de Hecho (Bal d'Echo in Aragonese).

Despite certain rights obtained by local authorities, even today only a small number of children learn Aragonese at kindergarten and school. Part of the problem is the small number of teachers trained to teach the language.

To end this section on the Romance language islands of the Iberian Peninsula, let's look at an excerpt from *The Little Prince* in two of the languages:

Mirandese:
Ah! Princepico, antendi als poucos la tue bidica triste. Durante muito tiempo, nun tubiste outra cousa que l ancanto de la çpousta de l sol para te çtraires. Soube-lo a la purmanhana de l quarto die, quando me deziste: Gusto muito de las çpoustas de l sol.

Aragonese:
Oi, prenzipet! Asinas, a moniquet, he entendiu a tuya chiqueta bida malinconica. Por muito tiempo a tuya unica entretenedera estió a suabura d'as clucadas de sol. M'enteré d'iste nuebo detalle o cuatreno día, de maitins, cuan me diziés: Me fa muito goyo as clucadas de sol..

Spanish:
¡Ah, principito! Así, poco a poco, comprendí tu pequeña vida melancólica. Durante mucho tiempo tu única distracción fue la suavidad de las puestas de sol. Me enteré de este nuevo detalle, en la mañana del cuarto día, cuando me dijiste: Me encantan las puestas de sol.

BRAZILIAN AND CHIPILO VENETIAN DIALECTS

The **Venetian** language (**łengoa vèneta** in Venetian) is a Romance language, spoken in the Italian region of **Veneto**, and to a lesser extent in the surrounding regions. It is an independent language, although many regard it as a dialect of Italian. Perhaps it would be most accurate to view Italian and Venetian as being two equal branches growing from a common **Vulgar Latin** tree. During the existence of the Venetian Republic, the Venetian language was the lingua franca of a large part of the Mediterranean region, but its importance declined sharply after the unification of Italy in the mid-nineteenth century.

The Venetian language does not have the status of an official language in Italy, but in fifteen municipalities of the southernmost Brazilian states, **Rio Grande do Sul** and **Santa Catarina**, Venetian and Portuguese are co-official!

BRAZILIAN VENETIAN/TALIAN

Brazilian Venetian, or **Talian**, is spoken by a large number of inhabitants of the southern states of **Rio Grande do Sul** and **Santa Catarina**, and also of the central coastal state of **Espírito Santo**. The Talian language is not a descendant of the Italian language, as could be inferred from the name. It is a language that emerged as a mixture of various dialects of the Veneto region and the surrounding Gallo-Italic languages, with the expected great influence of Portuguese, the official language of Brazil.

Statistics say that in Rio Grande do Sul, three million people (a third of the population) are of Italian origin. In the state of Espírito Santo, the percentages are even higher: there are 1.7 million Italians, or 70 per cent of the population. Unfortunately, many do not know the Venetian language, but the number of speakers is still large. Newspapers and radio stations in Talian certainly help.

Wine production is one of the most important industries for people of Italian origin in Brazil. The city of **Bento Gonçalves** (122,000 inhabitants) in the state of Rio Grande do Sul is especially famous for this. Not far from Bento Gonçalves is one of the richest cities in Brazil – **Caxias do Sul** (520,000 inhabitants), probably the most important Italian centre in the country, with a developed wine production, as well as industry and trade.

Wine fountain in the centre of Bento Gonçalves

CHIPILO VENETIAN

In 1882, several hundred migrants from the town of Segusino in the Italian region of Veneto finally established their new settlement – **Chipilo** in the Mexican state of Puebla, 90 kilometres southeast of the federal capital, Mexico City. The altitude of 2,150 metres helped to make their dairy products highly valued in much of Mexico. Despite the proximity of the city of Puebla, the capital of the state of the same name, **chipileños** (the Spanish name for the residents of Chipilo) have managed to largely maintain their **Chipilo Venetian** language to this day, as well as numerous cultural traditions. This is unusual, because most European immigrants quickly merged with Mexican culture, completely adopting Spanish.

In comparing the Venetian language spoken today in Italy and Mexico, it is apparent that **Italian Venetian** has been far more influenced by its surrounding languages than Chipilo Venetian. Despite the chipileños' frequent contact with Spanish and Aztec speakers from the surrounding settlements, the Chipilo Venetian language has changed minimally, with the exception of expected loanwords. It may seem odd then, given the lack of Spanish influence, that chipileños today most often use Spanish-based orthography to write their language, as it is actually more suited to Venetian than Italian-based orthography.

Chipilo has about 3,500 inhabitants, of whom 2,500 speak the Venetian language. Smaller colonies of speakers of this language are located in two other Mexican states: **Veracruz** and **Querétaro**. Many old customs are popular in all places inhabited by the descendants of Italians, such as the displaying of dolls representing *Befana*. Befana is usually presented as an (old) woman who brings presents to children on Twelfth Night or Epiphany Eve (the night of 5 January), in a similar way to Santa Claus. Children who have been good can expect to find sweets or toys in their socks, while the other children will only get a piece of charcoal.

Befana in Chipilo, Puebla, Mexico

CELTIC LANGUAGE ISLANDS

The **Celts** belong to the Indo-European peoples who began their expansion across the European continent during the sixth century BC from a relatively small area north of the Alps. At the time of the greatest territorial expansion, in the third century BC, they occupied vast areas of Europe, including Spain, Western and Central Europe, the British Isles, areas along the Danube and all the way to the central parts of Asia Minor.

Today, Celtic languages are used in only a few small areas of northwestern Europe, and each of these languages is a minority language in its own country, although great efforts are being made to preserve the language and increase the number of speakers. **Welsh** is the only living Celtic language that is not considered to be endangered. The Celtic languages are divided into two major groups:

- **Continental Celtic** languages, which were once spoken throughout Europe and Asia Minor. These languages are grouped purely on a geographical basis, since it is not known how they were related linguistically, nor to which group they originally belonged. All languages from this group are now extinct. The easternmost of them was **Galatian**, which was spoken in Asia Minor from the third century BC to the fourth or even sixth century AD.

- **Insular Celtic** languages, which are spoken today in increasingly small areas of the British Isles and the Brittany peninsula in France. This group of Celtic languages is further divided into two more groups: languages derived from **Middle Irish** (**Irish, Scottish Gaelic** and **Manx**) are classed as Goidelic, and languages derived from the **Common Brittonic** (**Welsh, Breton** and **Cornish**) are classed as Brittonic.

ATLANTIC

OCEAN

North

Sea

BARVAS

ARDNAMURCHAN

MEATH
GAELTACHT

Irish
Sea

MANX

UNITED

KINGDOM

IRELAND

AELTACHT NA NDÉISE

Celtic
Sea

CORNISH

English Channel

BRETON

FRANCE

ATLANTIC

OCEAN

Bay of
Biscay

IRISH LANGUAGE ISLANDS

When it comes to the linguistic islands of the **Irish** (or **Irish Gaelic**) language, a sad fact must be immediately pointed out: in its own independent state, the Irish language is a linguistic island (or, at best, a linguistic archipelago)! This conclusion is supported by the statistics, which show that the language is used regularly by only 10 per cent of the Irish population, and that less than 40 per cent has some solid knowledge of the language. *Gaeltacht* is the word used to describe a region in which Irish (**Gaeilge**) is the vernacular speech. Initially, these were areas where at least 25 per cent of the population spoke Irish, but today that percentage is often significantly lower. Most of the Gaeltacht regions are located on the west coast of Ireland, but we will look at two smaller Irish language islands, one of which is located in the south, the other in the east.

Gaeltacht na nDéise is located in the south of Ireland and consists of two villages: **Ring** and **Old Parish**. Ring, the larger of the two villages, has about 1,000 inhabitants. Of that number, a third speak Irish on all occasions. All levels of education (kindergarten, primary school and secondary school) in Ring are conducted entirely in Irish. The smaller of the two villages in this Gaeltacht is Old Parish, located not far from Ring, with just over 700 inhabitants. Only 15 per cent of Old Parish residents speak Irish. Since 2005, only the Irish names have been used for all settlements: *An Rinn* instead of Ring, *An Seanphobal* instead of Old Parish.

Some 50 kilometres northwest of the Irish capital Dublin (Baile Átha Cliath in Irish) is the smallest Gaeltacht – the **Meath Gaeltacht**. It is estimated that about 1,800 Irish-speaking people live in the area, which consists of two unconnected villages, **Baile Ghib** (**Gibstown** in English) and **Ráth Chairn** (**Rathcarran** in English). Unlike the other Gaeltacht, this one was created as a result of state *Gaelicization*, with the aim of returning the Irish language to the east of the island. In the mid-1930s, a large number of Irish speakers settled in these two villages (and several more, though they have since been deserted or else the Irish language has been replaced by English). The desire of the state authorities – to 'spread' the Irish language to the neighbouring villages – not only failed, but it led to almost all inhabitants of Baile Ghib and Ráth Chairn becoming largely bilingual.

■ Gaeltacht

ATLANTIC

OCEAN

NORTHERN
IRELAND
(UK)

BELFAST

Irish
Sea

MEATH
GAELTACHT

IRELAND

DUBLIN

GAELTACHT
NA NDÉISE

Celtic Sea

SCOTTISH GAELIC LANGUAGE ISLANDS

Scottish Gaelic (Gàidhlig) is a language spoken by part of the Scottish population, known as the **Gaels** of Scotland. After the kingdom of **Dál Riata** (or **Dalriada**) was created during the fourth and fifth centuries – which included islands and a small part of the mainland in the west of Scotland, and the northern parts of Northern Ireland – the way to Scotland was opened to Middle Irish, where it eventually formed Scottish Gaelic.

There is evidence, particularly in the names of numerous locations, that the Gaelic language was once spoken across almost the whole of Scotland. Despite this, just over one per cent of Scots speak Gaelic today. Great efforts are being made to renew the use of the language, but for now the main positive result is that the number of young speakers is no longer in decline.

The **Outer Hebrides** (**Na h-Eileanan Siar** in Scottish Gaelic) is an island chain located off the west coast of Scotland. It has a total population of 27,000, and the most important town is **Stornoway** (**Steòrnabhagh** in Scottish Gaelic) on the Isle of Lewis, with about 8,000 inhabitants, of which 45 per cent are Scottish Gaelic speakers. Stornoway is also the venue for the annual *Hebridean Celtic Festival* (*HebCelt*), an international Scottish music festival.

Overall, the number of Scottish Gaelic speakers is declining year by year, so that today there is no civil parish in which more than 65 per cent are speakers – **Barvas** (**Barabhas** in Scottish Gaelic) on the Isle of Lewis, has 64 per cent – and not a single one on the mainland of Scotland with more than 20 per cent – the 'champion' is **Ardnamurchan** (**Àird nam Murchan** in Scottish Gaelic) with 19 per cent.

The Canadian province of Nova Scotia, and especially its island of **Cape Breton**, has a number of Gaelic speakers. In the nineteenth century, Gaelic (or **Canadian Gaelic**) was the third most important European language on this continent, just behind English and French. Unfortunately, today its significance is much lower – across the whole of Nova Scotia and the neighbouring province of **Prince Edward Island**, there are only 2,000 speakers. Numerous efforts are being made to revive the use of the Gaelic language, such as the education of adults and the printing of useful books, as well as the use of Gaelic in several secondary schools.

MANX

The **Manx** language (**Gaelg** or **Gailck** in Manx) was spoken on the **Isle of Man** until 1974, when the last speaker died. After that, Manx was no longer officially or publicly used, although partial knowledge of the language survived in many households. The process of reviving the Manx language began in the middle of the twentieth century, so today about 1,800 people on the island have knowledge at the level of a second language.

Irish Gaelic, Scottish Gaelic and Manx are all derived from the Middle Irish language. The first two languages originated directly from this ancestor, while the strong influence of the Norse language on Middle Irish created today's Manx.

CORNISH

The **Cornish** language (**Kernewek** or **Kernowek** in Cornish) is a Celtic language from the Brittonic group, spoken on the **Cornwall** peninsula. It largely became extinct in the eighteenth century, although there is evidence that it continued to be used during much of the nineteenth century. It is believed that the process of revival began in 1904, with the publication of the book *A Handbook of the Cornish Language*. Today, there are about 500 people who speak Cornish as a second language, and about 3,000 people with basic knowledge. UNESCO removed Cornish from the list of extinct languages in 2010, but a huge effort is still needed to keep it off the list in future.

Giving Cornish names to children, boats and pets is becoming increasingly popular. Cornish is taught in some schools, and there are a number of media in which texts in the Cornish language can be read or heard.

WELSH LANGUAGE ISLANDS

Welsh is the only language among the Celtic languages that is not considered to be endangered. It belongs to the Brittonic group of Celtic languages, and today is spoken by over 800,000 people in **Wales**, or 30 per cent of the population. The government of Wales aims to have one million Welsh speakers by 2050, and the growing number of children attending school in their mother tongue raises hopes that this significant target could indeed be reached in the next thirty years.

As for the Welsh language island, it is not located in Wales, nor in the British Isles. It is not found in Europe, nor even in the northern hemisphere. The Welsh language island, known as **Y Wladfa** ('the colony') is located in the Argentine part of **Patagonia**. The colony began its life in 1865, when the Argentine government invited migrants from European countries to settle what even today is sparsely populated Patagonia. The Welsh built their settlements in the province of **Chubut**, in the east, along the Atlantic coast, and in the west, on the slopes of the magnificent Andes. Today's estimate of **Patagonian Welsh** speakers (**Cymraeg y Wladfa** in Welsh) puts the number at 2,000–5,000, all of whom are bilingual (Welsh/Spanish) or trilingual (Welsh/Spanish/English). The Welsh language has undergone some changes in Argentina, primarily numerous borrowings from Spanish, which has resulted in a new language, though still almost completely understandable to compatriots from Europe. One unexpected change occurred in Wales via the Patagonian Welsh: they learnt the decimal number system in Argentina, and later transferred it to Wales, where the previous vigesimal system (number system based on twenty) was duly replaced.

The main centres of Welsh culture in Argentina today are the cities of **Gaiman**, not far from the Atlantic coast of Argentina, and **Trevelin** (**Trefelin** in Welsh), in the Andes, just a few kilometres from the border with Chile.

Original flag of Y Wladfa with the wingless Welsh dragon

BRETON LANGUAGE ISLANDS

In truth, the **Breton** language (**Brezhoneg** in Breton) does not have any linguistic islands, but it can be said that the whole language is a kind of island. The reason is this: the Breton language is an Insular Celtic language, which is not spoken on the island (meaning Great Britain), but on the (European) Continent. Although all continental Celtic languages have long since become extinct, Breton is still alive on the Continent. So why is it classed as an Insular Celtic language? The reason is simple: Anglo-Saxon migrations to Britain forced some groups of Celts to leave their homes and flee to the continental mainland, from which they had moved to the island centuries earlier.

The Breton language belongs to the Brittonic group of Insular Celtic languages. Its closest relative is Cornish, with many scholars believing that they are merely two dialects of the same language. The Welsh and the extinct **Cumbric** – which was spoken in what are now Northern England and Lowland Scotland – are somewhat distant relatives from the same group of Celtic languages.

The homeland of the Breton language is **Brittany**, in northwest France, where it is being used less and less. In the middle of the twentieth century it was spoken by a million **Bretons**, while by the beginning of the twenty-first century that number had dropped to about 200,000 (with only 35,000 using the language in everyday speech), so UNESCO placed it into the 'endangered languages' group. The reason for this was the growing political centralization of France, as well as the significant influence of the media on the French language. An interesting fact is that parents were given the right to give their children Breton names only at the end of the twentieth century.

The city of Vannes (Gwened in Breton)
in southern Brittany

SIMILARITIES AND DIFFERENCES IN CELTIC LANGUAGE ISLANDS

The Little Prince can show us the similarities and differences between the Celtic languages:

Irish:
Maise, a phrionsa bhig, a stór, fuair mé tuigbhéail de réir a chéile don chumha a bhí ort i do shaol beag scoite. Ní raibh de chaitheamh aimsire ar feadh i bhfad ach an ghrian ag dul faoi agus a cineáltacht. Fuair mé an sonra nua seo amach ar maidin an cheathrú lá nuair a dúirt tú: Is maith liom an ghrian ag dul faoi.

Scottish Gaelic:
O, a phrionnsa bhig! Beag is beag thuig mi mar a bha do bheatha bheag dhubhach. Fad ùine mhòr cha robh dibhearsain agad ach a bhith a' coimhead caoineachas dol fodha na grèine. B' e rud ùr a bha sin a fhuair mi a-mach air madainn a' cheathramh latha, nuair a thuirt thu rium: Is fìor thoil leam dol fodha na grèine.

Manx:
O Phrince Veg! Ny vegganyn hooar mee briaght er folliaghtyn dty vea ôney hrimshagh. Ry-foddey dy hraa cha r'ou goaill taitnys ayns red erbee er-lhimmey jeh lhie ny greïney. Hooar mee shen magh er moghrey yn wheiggoo laa, tra dooyrt oo rhym: Ta mee feer ghraihagh er jeeaghyn er y ghrian goll sheese.

Welsh:
Dywysog bach! O dipyn i beth felly fe ddes i ddeall dy fywyd bach trist di. Doeddet ti ddim wedi cael dim i'th ddifyrru di ers amser ond mwynder machlud yr haul. Fe ddysgais i'r ffaith newydd hon ar fore'r pedwerydd diwrnod, pan ddwedaist wrthyf i: Rwy'n hoffi machlud yr haul.

Cornish:

A! Pennsevik byhan, my re gonvedhas, tamm ha tamm, dha vewnans byhan moredhek. Dres termyn hir nyns esa dhis didhan vyth marnas medhelder sedhesow an howl. My a dhyskas an manylyon nowyth ma, myttinweyth y'n peswara dydh, pan leversys dhymm: Da yw genev sedhesow an howl.

Breton:

A! priñs bihan, komprenet 'm eus, tamm-ha-tamm, da vuhezig velkonius. E-pad pell ne 'z poa bet evel didu nemet c'hwekted ar c'huzh-heol. Desket 'm eus ar munud nevez-se d'ar pevare deiz, d'ar beure, pa 'c'h eus lavaret din: Me 'blij din ar c'huzh-heol.

A FEW OTHER INDO-EUROPEAN LANGUAGE ISLANDS

ALBANIAN LANGUAGE ISLANDS

Albanian is an independent branch of the Indo-European language tree, without any known connection to any other language, living or extinct. There are several theories about the origin of this language, but it definitely developed from some or more Paleo-Balkan languages (**Illyrian** languages, **Thracian** or **Daco-Moesian**, all poorly known). Today, it is spoken by about 8 million people in Albania and a large diaspora. Some of the Albanian language islands are:

- The city of **Zadar**, a well-known summer resort on the Croatian Adriatic coast, where one suburb is named **Arbanasi** after the many inhabitants of Albanian ethnic origin (*Arbanasi* being an arhaic name for Albanians).

- The village of **Mandritsa** in southern Bulgaria, on the border with Greece. Today, only seventy (mostly elderly) people live in the village, most of whom speak Albanian.

- Some Albanian families left Mandritsa and settled in the village of **Mandres**, 30 kilometres north of Thessaloniki.

About 10,000 descendants of Albanians who reached Egypt as Ottoman soldiers in the eighteenth and nineteenth centuries still live in war-torn Syria. None of them speak Albanian.

ARVANITIKA

At the southern end of the Balkan Peninsula, around ancient **Athens** and on the **Peloponnese** peninsula in Greece, there are a large number of members of the **Arvanites** ethnic community. They speak the language of **Arvanitika** (**arbërisht** in Arvantika), and call themselves **Arbëreshë**. According to various estimates (Greece does not recognize the existence of national minorities, so this question is not asked in the censuses), today they number between 50,000 and 200,000, practically all of whom are assimilated into Greek society. In fact, most Arvanites would be offended if someone suggested they were not Greek, and many were at the forefront of the struggle to liberate Greece from Ottoman rule.

Arvanites originate from today's Albania, immigrating to Greece in the fifteenth century. Arvanitika is an endangered language, because most of the young people have switched to speaking **Greek**, without the desire or ability to pass on their mother tongue to their children.

ARBËRESH

Another, larger, group of Albanians fled before the invasion of the mighty Ottoman Empire in the fifteenth century, across the sea to **Southern Italy**. Today, the group numbers over 250,000, living in fifty villages in the south of the Apennine Peninsula and in Sicily. Of this number, about 100,000 ethnic **Arbëreshë** people speak their old language, known as **Arbëresh**. Unlike their compatriots from Greece, Italian Albanians proudly acknowledge their origins, while at the same time expressing Italian patriotism.

Most of the Italian Albanians today belong to the Italo-Albanian Church, an autonomous church that fully adheres to the old Byzantine (Orthodox) Church rites, but which recognizes the Pope as the supreme head.

Lungro is an important national and religious centre of the Italo-Albanians in the region of Calabria, located in the largest Italian national park, Pollino National Park. The city was founded at the end of the fifteenth century by refugees from what is today southern Albania. Most of the 3,500 inhabitants are Arbëreshë people, and the Arbëresh language is regularly used for all purposes.

Another important centre of the Italo-Albanians is the town of **Piana degli Albanesi** (**Hora e Arbëreshëvet** in Arbëresh) in the western part of Sicily. With over 6,000 inhabitants, Piana degli Albanesi is today the most important Arbëreshë centre in Sicily and the largest settlement of Italo-Albanians in all of Italy. For more than five centuries, the inhabitants have managed to preserve the language of their ancestors, as well as a large number of their customs. Piana degli Albanesi is a completely bilingual place, where almost all traffic and other signs are written in both Italian and Italo-Albanian; both languages are used in local schools and the media.

Of the fifty Arbëreshë villages, two in particular stand out: **Vaccarizzo Albanese** and **San Giorgio Albanese** (respectively, **Vakarici** and **Mbuzati** in Arbëresh). In these two villages, located on the sole of the Italian 'boot', 3,000 people speak a special dialect of the Arbëresh language, known as **Vaccarizzo Albanian** or **Calabria Arbëresh**. This speech is distinct for having a very large number of archaisms, and also for the fact that it contains many characteristics of the **Gheg** dialect from northern Albania, even though it originates from the **Tosk** dialect of southern Albania.

Belt buckle on an Arbëreshë costume worn in Piana degli Albanesi, Sicily

ALBANIANS IN UKRAINE

Ga tantë ('from ours') speak the language **si neve** ('like us') and live mainly in **Budzhak** and **Zaporizhzhia**, the southern coastal areas of Ukraine. As the title of this section suggests, these are the names used by Albanians, living in Ukraine, to describe their ethnic community and language.

In order to escape pressure from the Turkish authorities, groups of Orthodox Albanians migrated to Bulgaria, then continued on with groups of Bulgarians and Gagauz (Orthodox people of Turkic origin) in the direction of the Danube Delta and the southern borders of the Russian Empire. In the early nineteenth century, Albanians founded their first settlement in present-day Ukraine, the village of **Karakurt** (the name comes from the Turkish name for the black widow, an extremely dangerous species of spider). Today, Karakurt has about 3,000 inhabitants, 60 per cent of whom are of Albanian origin (25 per cent are Bulgarian and 10 per cent are Gagauz), and the use of the Albanian language is very evident.

In the second half of the nineteenth century, some of the Albanians from Karakurt decided to move further east, so in Zaporizhzhia, near the Sea of Azov, they built several small villages – **Heorhiivka**, **Hamivka** and **Divnynske** – where you can still hear the Albanian language today, and also visit museums of local Albanian culture. Although the Albanian language in Albania is written in Latin script, Ukrainian Albanians usually use Cyrillic to write their language. There is no Albanian school in Ukraine.

ARMENIAN LANGUAGE ISLANDS

The **Armenian** language consists of two mutually intelligible spoken and written forms: **Eastern** and **Western Armenian.** The Eastern Armenian language is based on the language of **Yerevan,** the Armenian capital, and is mostly used today in Armenia, the former Soviet Union and Iran. The Western Armenian language is based on the speech of Armenians from what is now **Turkey;** it is the main language of the Armenian diaspora, a consequence of the *Armenian genocide* of 1915, when the forces of the Ottoman Empire forcibly displaced and eliminated between 800,000 and 1,500,000 Armenians. The surviving Armenians scattered throughout the Middle East, Europe and North America, taking with them the Western Armenian language. The Republic of Turkey denies that there was any Armenian genocide at all. Apart from the diaspora, the Western Armenian language, more specifically the **Karin** dialect, is also spoken in the northwestern regions of Armenia and the southern parts of Georgia. Some small Armenian language islands are the towns of **Aikavan** (**Haykavan** in Armenian) in Crimea and **Edissiya** in Russia, as well as the **Sokhumi** district, which is part of Abkhazia, Georgia's breakway province.

VAKIFLI, TURKEY

The village of **Vakıflı** is the only remaining wholly Armenian village in Turkey, located on the slopes of Musa Dagh mountain (Musa ler in Armenian: 'Moses Mountain') on the Mediterranean coast close to the Turkish–Syrian border. It was its location that enabled the village of Vakıflı to survive the bloody year of 1915, when the Armenians settled on this inaccessible mountain, fiercely defending themselves for fifty-three days from strong Turkish attacks. During the battles, the Armenians hung a large banner on the trees on the side of the mountain facing the sea, which was seen by sailors on several French ships. An agreement was reached with the French, and the Armenian population of Musa Dagh was transferred by boat to a safe location. After the conflict, residents of seven Armenian villages were returned to their homes, while the area, known as the province of **Hatay**, remained under French rule, guaranteeing security for the Christian population, which included the Armenians.

However, the situation changed in 1939, when France handed Hatay over to Turkey, hoping to win Turkey over in the months before the outbreak of the Second World War. The Turkish ownership of Musa Dagh meant another migration for the residents of six Armenian villages, this time to the Bekaa Valley in eastern Lebanon, where they founded the Armenian city of **Anjar**. The inhabitants of the seventh village, Vakıflı (**Vak'yf** in Armenian), did not want to leave their houses again, so this village remained the only Armenian village in all of Turkey, although at the beginning of the twentieth century, there were still several million Armenians living on Turkish soil.

Today, 130 Armenians live in Vakıflı, speaking a specific dialect of the West Armenian language, which is difficult for other speakers of this Armenian language to understand.

ANJAR, LEBANON

In eastern Lebanon, the town of **Anjar** (also known as **Aanjar** and **Haouch Moussa**) in the Bekaa Valley is located in the most important agricultural area of this Middle Eastern country. Historical sources say that a town was founded at this site in the eighth century, but that it was abandoned around the turn of the twentieth century. The town then lay empty until the influx of the thousands of Armenian refugees from Musa Dagh in 1939, who named some parts of the town after the abandoned villages of their old homeland. The town has almost 2,500 inhabitants today, the vast majority of whom are Armenian.

During the 1960s, Anjar made good progress, but that progress was later slowed down by the outbreak of civil war in Lebanon. After the end of the civil war, Anjar resumed its accelerated development, and became an example to the whole of Lebanon as a place with a very low crime rate, clean air and a high standard of living. Today, there are several Armenian churches and schools in the city, and the Armenian language is intensively used for all purposes. It is interesting to note that Anjar has its own police force, which reports directly to the town administration, and not to the Lebanese Interior Ministry, as is the case in other cities.

Historic stone arches in ancient Anjar, Lebanon

FEREYDAN, IRAN

A large number of Armenians living in the **Fereydan** area of the central Iranian province of Isfahan (also written as Eşfahān) are the descendants of people from Nakhchivan (Naxçıvan in Azeri), today's Azerbaijani enclave located between Armenia, Iran and Turkey. Shah Abbas the Great expelled the people from Nakhchivan in the seventeenth century, forcing them from their homes in the town of Julfa (Culfa in Azeri, Jugha in Armenian), as punishment for a rebellion (Julfa is best known for its huge Armenian cemetery, which was destroyed after the collapse of the Soviet Union). Today, there is only one ethnically homogeneous Armenian village – **Zarneh** in Persian, **Boloran** in Armenian – with about sixty inhabitants, located 150 or so kilometres west of Isfahan city.

There is an Armenian quarter in Isfahan, known as **New Julfa** in honour of the place from where the first Armenians hailed. According to estimates, slightly more than 10,000 Armenians live in Isfahan today (the city as a whole has more than 1.5 million inhabitants), and there is an Armenian school, a large number of Armenian churches, museums and other facilities in New Julfa. Armenians in this neighbourhood fully respect Iranian regulations and customs regarding dress code, but they use their language and tradition, protected by Iranian laws and authorities, without any issues.

Depiction of Heaven, Earth and Hell inside the Holy Savior Cathedral, New Julfa, Isfahan, Iran

KASSAB, SYRIA

Kassab (also spelled **Kessab**) is a town on the northern Syrian coast, on the border with Turkey. It is mostly inhabited by people of Armenian heritage. For this town, as well as for many other places inhabited by those of Armenian descent, the twentieth century began very badly: in 1909, the *Adana massacre* took place, when over 20,000 Armenians and other Christians were killed in the southern Turkish city of **Adana** and its surroundings, including Kassab. Only six years later, the Armenian genocide began. During this time, a huge number of Armenians from Kassab and the surrounding area were forced to march to their deaths, with entire families being marched through the Syrian and Jordanian deserts. More than 5,000 people lost their lives during those marches.

Most of the villages around Kassab are inhabited largely by Armenians, who speak a special dialect of the West Armenian language. There are several schools in Kassab where classes are conducted in the Armenian language. According to statistics, 2,500 people live in Kassab and its surrounding villages today, of whom 80 per cent are Armenians and 20 per cent are Arab Alawites.

Before the Syrian civil war began in 2011, Kassab was one of the favourite summer resorts for many residents of Aleppo and Latakia due to the rich green forests in the hills and valleys around the town.

GLENDALE, CALIFORNIA, UNITED STATES

On the other side of the world, just 15 kilometres north of downtown Los Angeles, is the city of **Glendale**. According to the census, out of a population of around 200,000, just over 65,000 of Glendale's inhabitants are of Armenian origin, and almost all of them use the Armenian language.

The first Armenians began to settle in this area of California in the mid-1920s, but the largest number arrived during the 1970s. Although Armenians are extremely well integrated in Glendale (and in all of Los Angeles in fact, where there are over 150,000 Armenians today), they have not forgotten their language or traditions. Several schools offer great help to children to master the language of their ancestors, while a number of cultural organizations keep ancient traditions alive. Today, Glendale is considered to be the second largest Armenian municipality in the world, right behind the Armenian capital of Yerevan.

Both the singer and bassist of the Armenian-American rock band *System of a Down*, Serj Tankian and Shavo Odadjian, lived in this 'Armenian capital of North America' for a while.

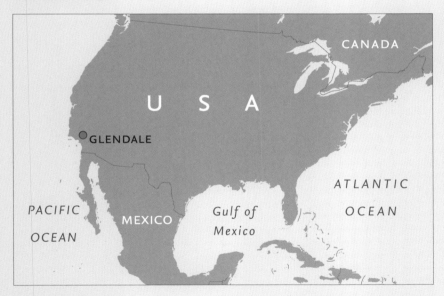

SAN LAZZARO DEGLI ARMENI, ITALY

San Lazzaro degli Armeni (**St Lazarus Island** in English) is an island of three hectares, located in a lagoon two kilometres away from the city of Venice. Since 1717, the monastery of San Lazzaro has occupied the island (during which time, land reclamation has increased the size of the island by almost four times).

St Lazarus Island is considered an extremely important centre of Armenian culture and the study of its language, even though only a very small number of monks live there (currently fewer than twenty, and as far as it is known, there have never been more than a hundred at a time). The first complete dictionary of the Armenian language and the first modern history of the Armenian people were compiled on this island during the eighteenth century.

The monks on the island also produce *vartanush*, a highly esteemed Armenian jam made from rose petals, using the many roses in the monastery garden. Most of this jam is eaten by the monks themselves, but some jars are sold in the monastery shop.

San Lazzaro degli Armeni, Venice, Italy

GREEK LANGUAGE ISLANDS

Greek, like Albanian and Armenian, is a separate branch of the Indo-European language tree. Of all the Indo-European languages, it has the longest written history – the oldest known text was written about 3,400 years ago. There are several Greek settlements that make up language islands, including:

- **Mariupol**, the main centre of the Greek language (**Mariupolitan Greek**, also known as **Rumeika**) and culture in Ukraine. In one village, **Anadol**, pure **Pontic Greek** is still spoken. In the vicinity of Mariupol, there are also **Urums**, who are Orthodox Greeks that speak **Urum**, the **Crimean Tatar** dialect!

- The village of **Beloiannisz**, which is located just a few kilometres south of Budapest, the capital of Hungary. The village was built by Greek volunteers in 1950. Out of a total of 1,200 inhabitants, approximately one quarter are Greek. The village is named after Nikos Beloyannis, one of the leaders of the Communist Party of Greece.

TSAKONIAN

The area along the east coast of the Peloponnese peninsula is called **Tsakonia**. It contains a dozen villages and towns where a large number of people speak the **Tsakonian** language. The Tsakonian language is classed as a Greek speech, though it is significantly different from all other Greek dialects. In fact, linguistically speaking, it could be regarded as a separate language, since it is almost completely incomprehensible to the speakers of today's modern Greek language.

The reason for the separation of the Tsakonian language lies in the ancient history of the Greek language. Around 1150 BC, the **Dorians**, a Greek tribe from the area of Epirus (today the border area of Greece and Albania), began their invasion of the south of Greece, all the way to the southern coast of the Peloponnese. They took their own dialect of the Greek language, known as **Doric Greek**, to the occupied territories. The most famous Greek city-state in which Doric Greek was spoken was **Sparta**. However, despite the strength of Sparta and other Doric allies, linguistic dominance was won by Athens, whose language – **Attic Greek** – became the basis of today's Greek language, while Doric languages eventually became extinct and disappeared... except in one small, isolated part of the Peloponnese! You guessed it: the Tsakonian language is today the only surviving descendant of the once widespread Doric Greek. Despite having survived for more than 2,000 years, Tsakonian today belongs to the group of endangered languages. One reason for this is the increased access to television and other modern media over the last few decades, making standard Greek readily available to these isolated and hidden villages.

The town of **Leonidio** (**Agie Lidi** in Tsakonian) is today considered the capital of Tsakonia, and an increasing number of tourists are enjoying the protected old buildings throughout the settlement, as well as the striking nature around it.

'Our language is Tsakonian. Ask people to speak it with you'
A bilingual (Tsakonian and standard Greek) sign, Leonidio, Greece

GRIKO

In the extreme south of the Italian 'boot', there are two more Greek-speaking islands, one at the very toes, the other in the heel. A large number of Greek speakers are located in a dozen towns in the heel, on the **Salentine Peninsula** (**Salento** in Italian), where almost a half of the 40,000 inhabitants speak the **Griko** dialect as their first language. This area is also known as **Grecìa Salentina**. The second (and much smaller) group of Greek settlements is located at the tip of the toes of the Italian boot, in the province of Calabria. Fewer than 2,000 speakers of the Greek dialect known as **Greko** inhabit a dozen villages in the area known as **Grecia Calabra**, or **Bovesia**. Both of these so-called **Italiot Greek** dialects are partially intelligible to speakers of standard Greek.

There are two theories about the origin of the Greeks in southern Italy (although probably the most accurate is a combination of them):

- Today's Italo-Greeks are descended from the settlers of the eighth century BC, when Greek city-states formed **Magna Graecia** ('Greater Greece'), numerous colonies in southern Italy and Sicily.

- The dialects were based on the Greek language from the time of the fall of Byzantium under the rule of the Ottoman Turks in the fifteenth century.

The Italian state recognizes the existence of the Greek language minority and its obligation to protect it, but in spite of this, UNESCO considers that Griko is critically endangered. From a cultural perspective, the good news is that songs, music and poetry in the Greek language are very popular in Italy and Greece. The Greeks from the 'heel' have come together to create *The Union of the Towns of Grecìa Salentina*, an association with the task of studying and protecting the language and culture of Griko speakers, holding Griko classes in schools and printing books in this endangered language.

GREEKS IN ROMANIA

The first Greek settlements within modern-day Romania were established in the seventh century BC, as colonies and trading offices of Greek city-states. At that time, the Greeks also founded **Tomis** (today the main Romanian port of Constanța), the oldest permanently inhabited city in Romania.

The most significant period for the Greeks in Romania was probably the eighteenth and nineteenth centuries, the so-called **Phanariote** era. The Phanariotes were members of wealthy Greek families based in Phanar (now Fener), part of Constantinople (now Istanbul), where the Ecumenical Patriarchate was located. Traditionally, the Phanariotes held several very important positions, including the rulers of the vassal principalities of Moldavia and Wallachia (until their unification into Romania, when the descendants of the Phanariotes continued to play important state and economic roles).

Today, fewer than 7,000 Greek-speaking people live in Romania; at the end of the twentieth century, there were 20,000 Greeks, which shows the speed of assimilation and emigration of this ethnic group. The place with the highest percentage of Greeks is the municipality of **Izvoarele**, not far from the Danube Delta. In this municipality, which consists of three villages, there are just over 2,000 people, 55 per cent Romanians and 45 per cent Greeks. The municipality was founded in 1828 by Greek refugees from Turkish Thrace (Doğu Trakya in Turkish) – the European part of Turkey – after a rebellion against Turkish rule. They began a new life there, building their own school and church. Despite the official use of the Greek language being banned by the communist dictator of Romania, Nicolae Ceaușescu, the inhabitants of Izvoarele have still managed to preserve their archaic speech.

AL HAMIDIYAH, SYRIA

For nearly 400 years following the fall of the **Byzantine Empire**, almost all of present-day Greece was under Turkish rule, until the establishment of the independent Kingdom of Greece in the first half of the nineteenth century. One of the territories that remained outside the newly created Greek kingdom was the large island of Crete.

In the second half of the nineteenth century, another uprising broke out on Crete, which at the end of that century escalated into bloody conflict between the Orthodox Greek population on one side, and the Turks and other Muslims on the other. These 'other Muslims' are crucial to this story. This group of Muslims on Crete represented the Greeks whose ancestors had accepted the Muslim faith, but who had retained the Greek language and the sense of belonging to the Greek ethnic community. The Orthodox Greeks considered them traitors and enemies, so they treated them that way. The Ottoman Sultan Abdul Hamid II realized that the Turkish rule over Crete had come to an end, so he ordered the withdrawal of the Turks and the 'other Muslims' from the island. Still today there is one place where the descendants of Cretan Muslims largely speak the **Cretan Greek** dialect. It is the town of **Al Hamidiyah** in Syria.

The town is located on the coast in the extreme south of Syria, almost on the border with Lebanon, and it was named in honour of its founder. Today, the town has a population of 8,000, of which at least 60 per cent regularly uses the Greek language for all communication. A large number of children have their first contact with Arabic, the official language of Syria, only at school. The fact that the island of Crete is relatively close to the Syrian coast allows Greeks from Al Hamidiyah to access Greek TV and radio programmes, which greatly facilitates maintaining a high level of knowledge of the mother tongue, although many words that are obsolete in standard Greek are used in speech, as well as borrowings from Arabic.

CAPPADOCIAN GREEK

In 1071, the Battle of Manzikert was fought not far from the Turkish–Iranian border between the Byzantine Empire and the (Turkish) **Seljuq Empire**. The outcome of this battle was the catastrophic defeat of Byzantium, one of the consequences of which was the rapid settlement of most of Anatolia by Turkish tribes. This further led to the physical separation of **Cappadocia** (the southeastern part of today's Turkey) from the rest of Greek-speaking Byzantium. The Greeks who had inhabited the area for centuries now found themselves under strong pressure from the new Turkish masters and their language. **Cappadocian Greek** was eventually created by mixing the Cappadocian dialect of Greek with Turkish.

After the agreed exchange of population between Greece and Turkey in 1923, all Christians from Turkey were transferred to Greece, while Greek Muslims were moved to Turkey. This population exchange also included the Cappadocian Greeks, who were mostly relocated to the northern parts of Greece. Since all schools, books, media and administration exclusively used modern Greek, Cappadocian Greek quickly became extinct in the early 1960s. Or so it was thought!

During a 2005 study, several researchers in northern Greece found that Cappadocian Greek is not extinct at all, but that almost 3,000 people regularly use this unusual Greek language in several villages along the northern Greek border. Another unusual thing was noticed: a large number of younger Cappadocian Greeks actually spoke their language better than their parents did! Two settlements with more speakers of Cappadocian Greek are **Mandra** near the city of Larissa and **Xirochori** near Thessaloniki.

Elia Kazan, one of the most important directors in Hollywood and on Broadway, was a Cappadocian Greek. In the 1963 film *America America*, Kazan depicts the hardships of Greek life in Cappadocia through the story of his uncle. The film is included in the annual selection of twenty-five notable films in the *National Film Registry* of the Library of Congress.

SANSKRIT LANGUAGE ISLANDS

The two most important Indian epics, the *Mahabharata* and the *Ramayana*, were written in **Epic Sanskrit**, which was used by writers and poets in northern India from the fourth century BC to the third century AD. The end of this period also marks the end of the development of Sanskrit as a living, spoken language, but its use continues within the framework of religious and customary rites throughout India and its neighbouring countries.

Today, Sanskrit (Saṃskṛtam in Sanskrit) is taught in a large number of schools in **India** and, interestingly, over the past few decades the inhabitants of several villages have decided to almost completely switch to the use of Sanskrit in everyday life. The result is that there are now a few villages in which Sanskrit is used for all private and official purposes.

Today, Sanskrit is one of the twenty-two languages with official status in India (these are known as the *scheduled languages*), while the two northern federal states of Himachal Pradesh and Uttarakhand have decided to make Sanskrit their second official language. The census reveals that today in India, with almost 1.4 billion inhabitants, 25,000 speakers regard Sanskrit as their mother tongue.

The villages of **Mattur** and **Hosahalli** are twin villages, located on opposite banks of the Tunga river almost in the very centre of the state of Karnataka. The inhabitants of both villages spoke **Kannada** and Tamil until the mid-1980s, when a local priest suggested that they switch to Sanskrit. They welcomed this suggestion, and so the greeting *Katham aasthi?* ('How are you?' in Sanskrit) is increasingly heard across the villages. With 5,000 inhabitants, Mattur is the most significant settlement in India in terms of the attempt to renew the Sanskrit language.

HINDI LANGUAGE ISLANDS

The **Hindustani** language is an Indo-European language, developed from the medieval dialects of Delhi and its surroundings, and whose basis was the ancient language of Sanskrit. Hindustani is a *polycentric* language (a language with more than one standardized form) consisting of two largely mutually intelligible standardized forms: the standard **Hindi** language and the standard **Urdu** language. Hindustani is the third most widely spoken language in the world, after **Mandarin** and English.

While India was under British rule, large numbers of Indians migrated to other colonies within the **British Empire**. In the late nineteenth and early twentieth centuries, tens of thousands of Indian workers were taken to the archipelago of **Fiji**, which was then a British colony. Most of these workers spoke northern Hindi dialects, primarily **Awadhi** and **Bhojpuri**, from which **Fiji Hindi** – the language spoken by most Indian Fijians today – was developed.

Frequent riots and military coups led to regular attacks on Indians in Fiji, causing large numbers to leave Fiji for Australia, New Zealand, Canada and the United States. Today, indigenous Fijians represent 55 per cent of the population of Fiji, and Indo-Fijians 38 per cent.

Sri Siva Subramaniya (the largest Hindu temple in the Pacific), Nadi, Fiji

Just as Indian workers travelled to the large sugar cane plantations in Fiji, they reached the Caribbean Islands and nearby coastal areas of South America in the same way. In time, another dialect of the Hindi language was created, known as **Caribbean Hindustani**. Having many different local names, this is the spoken language in:

- **Guyana**, where a number of the 300,000 local Indians use **Guyanese Hindustani**, also known as **Aili Gaili**

- **Trinidad and Tobago**, where 15,000 people speak **Trinidadian Hindustani** or **Gaon ke Bolee** ('village speech'). Approximately 10,000 Indians in Trinidad and Tobago speak standard Hindi, and an increasing number also use **Hinglish** ('Hindu' + 'English')

- **Suriname**, where **Sarnami (Surinamese) Hindustani** is used for unofficial purposes by the Indo-Surinamese, who make up just over a quarter of Suriname's population

Monument dedicated to the first Indian settlers, Paramaribo, Suriname

Mauritius is an island nation in the Indian Ocean, about 2,000 kilometres from the east coast of Africa and 900 kilometres from Madagascar. Just like Fiji and the Caribbean, Mauritius was also known for its plantations, on which a large number of Indians worked. Today, only 5 per cent of the population of Mauritius speaks Bhojpuri, the Hindi dialect from northern India; most of these speakers belong to the older generation, especially in the rural areas of the island.

Mauritian banknote with central text in English, Tamil and Bhojpuri

Another destination for Indians during the nineteenth century was **South Africa**, which was also part of the British Empire at the time. Among them was a significant number of educated people, including doctors and lawyers. One of these lawyers would later become known as perhaps the greatest human rights activist. This was Mohandas Karamchand Gandhi, who, thanks to his advocacy for the rights of the poor and disenfranchised people of South Africa, was given the famous nickname *Mahātmā* (Sanskrit for 'great-souled').

Today, the Indian South African population stands at about 1.5 million, which is mostly concentrated in KwaZulu-Natal province. In several cities, the majority population is of Indian origin. Two of these are **Phoenix** (85 per cent of the total population of 180,000) and **oThongathi** (57 per cent of the 43,000 inhabitants), which is the oldest Indian settlement in South Africa, founded in 1860 for workers of a nearby sugar cane plantation.

YAGHNOBI

Sogdia was an ancient Iranian civilization, which included parts of today's Tajikistan, Uzbekistan, Kyrgyzstan and the southernmost region of Kazakhstan. The penetration of Islam into the Sogdian city-states replaced the hitherto dominant religious teachings in this area (primarily Zoroastrianism) with a new religion. Along with the new religion came a new language – **Persian** – which eventually replaced the **Sogdian** language.

However, small groups of Sogdian people, determined to avoid the violence that often accompanied a change of religion, found refuge in the high and isolated valleys of what is now central and western Tajikistan. Their descendants eventually embraced Islam, but nevertheless continued to use a modern variant of the Sogdian language, the **Yaghnobi** language.

Yaghnobi people

Yaghnobi (yaɣnobí zivók in Yaghnobi) is an **Eastern Iranian** language, spoken today in parts of western Tajikistan and several smaller areas near its capital, Dushanbe. Today there are about 13,000 Yaghnobis, originating from the **Yaghnob Valley** area, which is about seventy kilometres north of Dushanbe and has an altitude of 2,500 to 3,000 metres.

Probably the most difficult period in the Yaghnobis' history occurred during the 1970s, when the Soviet authorities – Tajikistan was part of the Soviet Union until 1990 – decided to forcibly displace them. The justification was that they were at risk from severe mountain avalanches. Their new home was **Zafarobod District**, a completely isolated region in northwestern Tajikistan, which today is home to about 6,500 Yaghnobis. It was only after Tajikistan's declaration of independence that a return to the Yaghnob valley was approved; fewer than 500 Yaghnobis accepted this, because their old homes had been destroyed by the Soviet army.

Yaghnobi children

LANGUAGE ISLANDS
AROUND THE WORLD

OCEANIA

Oceania covers a large geographical region that includes Australia, New Zealand and most of the islands of the Pacific Ocean, which are grouped into three great subregions: Melanesia, Micronesia and Polynesia. What connects all of these areas is the Pacific, the world's largest ocean.

A large number of languages are spoken across Oceania. The most widely used are the languages of the colonial powers – primarily English and French – while most of the others are grouped into three large families:

- **Austronesian** languages (390 million speakers), a language family that stretches from Madagascar, through Insular Southeast Asia and smaller parts of Taiwan to the countless islands of the Pacific. The largest language in this family is **Malay**, spoken by 290 million people in Malaysia, Indonesia, Brunei and Singapore.

- **Australian Aboriginal** languages, of which there were approximately 300 before the colonization of Australia by Europeans, while today there are fewer than 150. Only twenty of these languages are now spoken by large numbers (a total of just over 50,000 people).

- The **Papuan** languages of the island of New Guinea and the smaller surrounding islands.

Among these numerous languages, there are several interesting language islands.

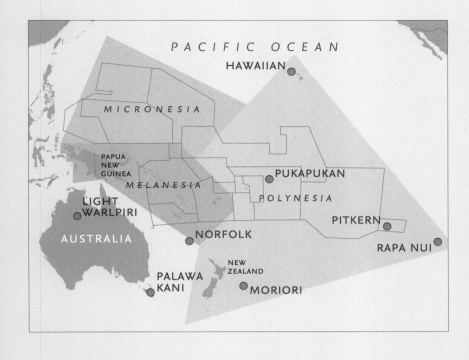

HAWAIIAN

The **Hawaiian** language (**ʻŌlelo Hawaiʻi** in Hawaiian) is an Austronesian language spoken by **Native Hawaiians** (**Kānaka Maoli** in Hawaiian) in the **Hawaiian Islands**, a large archipelago in the North Pacific Ocean. It is assumed that the ancestors of today's Hawaiians reached Hawaii around the year 1300 from the Society Islands (now part of French Polynesia) in the South Pacific. Fewer than 25,000 Hawaiians speak the Hawaiian language, although English and Hawaiian are the official languages of the US State of Hawaii.

Niʻihau is the westernmost and smallest of the seven inhabited Hawaiian Islands. It has been privately owned since the mid-nineteenth century and is known by the nickname *The Forbidden Isle*. The reason for this is simple and quite obvious: only persons with the permission of the owner can set foot on the island, as well as military and state personnel.

According to the 2010 census, 170 people live on the island of Niʻihau (area: 180 square kilometres). Residents speak the **Niʻihau** dialect of the Hawaiian language. Due to the isolation of the island, the Niʻihau dialect is most similar to the original Hawaiian language from before the first contact with Europeans.

In the only settlement on the island, Puʻuwai ('heart' in Hawaiian), there is a one-roomed schoolhouse with twenty to thirty pupils of all ages. During primary education, the Niʻihau dialect is used, while later, Hawaiian and English are used equally. The school is supplied with electricity through solar energy because there is no electricity network on the island. Also, there are no telephone lines or paved roads, and the main means of transport is by horse or bicycle. There is no sewage network, and the inhabitants of the island catch rainwater for their water supply. There are no hotels, and the few visitors are forbidden contact with the local population. As well as this, residents do not pay rent, and they receive meat for free.

It is interesting to note that many Hawaiians use **Hawaiian Creole English** (or **Hawaiian Pidgin**), abbreviated as HCE, in everyday casual speech. This is a language or dialect of English created by mixing English and Hawaiian. The number of HCE speakers is significantly higher than the number of remaining Hawaiian speakers – about 600,000 at the first language level and another 400,000 at the second language level.

The Little Prince, which has been used many times in this book, can serve as an example of a text in Hawaiian dialects:

Hawaiian:

Auē! e ke keiki ali'i li'ili'i, 'ano maopopo nō ia'u i kēia manawa ka minamina o kou ola. 'A'ole i lō'ihi loa kou nanea 'ana i ka nani o ka napo'o 'ana o ka lā. Ua a'o wau i kēia 'ike hou i ka 'ahā o ka lā i kakahiaka, i kou wā i 'ōlelo mai ai ia'u: Makemake nōwau i ka napo'o 'ana o ka lā.

Hawaiian Creole English:

Kay den, small prince, so I had catch, slow by slow, how sad yo life. You neva have long time fo enjoy da sunsets. I had learn dis on da fourt morning when you had tell me: Ho, you know me, I love sunsets.

Ni'ihau, The Forbidden Isle

PITKERN-NORFOLK

When Master's Mate Fletcher Christian started the *Mutiny on the Bounty* on 28 April 1789, he probably did not think that this would lead to the birth of a new language!

The ship HMS *Bounty* set out from England for the South Pacific island of Tahiti in the late eighteenth century, on a mission to take breadfruit tree seedlings from there to Jamaica. After a few months of rest on Tahiti, the sailors were reluctant to leave the paradise beaches and the Tahitian hospitality. Soon after they left, a revolt broke out on board, led by Fletcher Christian, causing HMS *Bounty* to return to Tahiti, where sixteen sailors left the ship, while nine rebels, thirteen Tahitian women and six Tahitian men continued eastwards to **Pitcairn Island**. The island was chosen very cunningly: on the nautical charts of the day, Pitcairn was plotted about 200 kilometres away from its true location, so the chance of a British ship finding the rebels was minimal.

The isolation of Pitcairn Island also meant that a new language emerged, which developed as a mixture of English and Tahitian languages from the eighteenth century. The language was named **Pitkern**, and today it is the main language of the island of Pitcairn, where it is taught in the only school and is spoken by all fifty inhabitants. However, a significantly larger number of speakers lives on **Norfolk Island**, far away from the rebel island where the language originated. The reason: in 1856, the British authorities realized that Pitcairn Island had become too small for its increased number of inhabitants, so the entire population (almost 200 people) was relocated. Over the following ten years, several families decided to return to Pitcairn, but even today, more than half of the population of Norfolk Island is descended from the HMS *Bounty* rebels.

On the Australian external territory of Norfolk Island, the language is called **Norf'k** (also **Norfuk** or **Norfolk**), and is spoken by about 1,000 people out of a total of 1,800 inhabitants. The Territory of Norfolk Island (Teratri a' Norf'k Ailen in Norf'k) is visited by many tourists, so the language is becoming diluted by English.

Pulau School, in Adamstown, is the only school on Pitcairn Island

RAPA NUI

Easter Island (**Rapa Nui** in the local **Rapa Nui** language) is a small, isolated Chilean island in the southeastern Pacific Ocean, known for its hundreds of imposing sculptures, the famous *moai*. The sculptures were erected by the ancestors of today's **Rapa Nui**, who sailed to the island in the early thirteenth century. In time, they created their own culture, mythology and tradition, and they have preserved their language to this day, although they have gone through various difficult moments in their history (including conflicts with Europeans, islanders being taken into Peruvian slavery, numerous deadly diseases...). Today, the island has about 6,000 inhabitants, of whom about 60 per cent are descendants of the indigenous Rapa Nui. Unfortunately, fewer than 1,000 of them speak Rapa Nui.

It is assumed that the Rapa Nui language was once written in a script known as **Rongorongo**. Despite several attempts, Rongorongo has not yet been deciphered, so it is not known whether it really is an alphabet or some form of record that merely resembles an alphabet. Today, there is not a single tablet bearing Rongorongo inscription located on the island of Rapa Nui, as they have all been taken into museums and private collections around the world.

One of the Rongorongo tablets, the so-called Tablet G or Small Santiago

PUKAPUKAN

The **Cook Islands** is a self-governing island nation in free association with New Zealand, which means that New Zealand is only responsible for defence and foreign affairs. The inhabitants of the Cook Islands, about 17,500 of them, speak English, **Cook Islands Māori** (a language very close to **New Zealand Māori**) and the **Pukapukan** language.

Pukapukan belongs to a large group of Austronesian languages, and developed on the very isolated island of **Pukapuka**, about 1,200 kilometres away from the main Cook Island of Rarotonga. In Pukapukan, the island that gives its name to the language is called *Te Ulu-o-Te-Watu* ('the head of the stone'), and the main settlement is called *Wale* ('home'). The total area of the island is 3 square kilometres, which is inhabited by fewer than 500 people. All of these speak the local language, and this has been taught in the island school since the 1980s.

The most interesting thing about the Pukapukan language concerns the names of colours. According to some information, names only exist for four colours: white, black, red and a combination of yellow, blue and green. The names of these colours actually come from the layers of roots of the taro (or talo) plant – the main source of food for the islanders – which are usually these colours.

The coral atoll of Pukapuka

LIGHT WARLPIRI

Warlpiri is a language from the **Pama-Nyungan** family, the largest Australian First Nation language family; it is spoken today by 3,000 members of the **Warlpiri** people, although there are at least twice as many members of this people. Members of the community inhabit a number of settlements and towns in the Northern Territory, north and west of the city of Alice Springs, and call themselves **Yapa**, meaning 'person'. However, one of these settlements, **Lajamanu**, stands out from all the others, because it is the only place where **Light Warlpiri** is spoken.

Light Warlpiri (**Warlpiri rampaku** in Light Warlpiri) is a mixed language, created by the younger generations of Lajamanu by merging the vocabulary and grammar rules of three languages: Warlpiri, English and Kriol. The language originated in the 1980s, so today there are already people for whom Light Warlpiri is the first language. Lajamanu has almost 700 inhabitants, and more than half regularly speak (but do not write) Light Warlpiri. These are primarily under the age of 40. Of course, everyone knows standard Warlpiri, and a large number know both Kriol and English.

The great distance of Lajamanu from other settlements influenced the creation of this new language, especially in the early days (those 'ancient' times before the Internet). The unique common language strengthened the young people's sense of belonging to the community, which has had a positive impact on the teaching of the language to their children.

As well as its distinctive language, Lajamanu is also known for being home to a large number of artists who exhibit their works on wood, stone and other materials both in a small, shared gallery and also throughout Australia.

PALAWA KANI

When the first Europeans reached the Australian island of **Tasmania** at the beginning of the nineteenth century, there were up to 10,000 Tasmanians living there. However, a period of violent conflict and the introduction of infectious diseases brought by the Europeans nearly wiped out this population in a short space of time. The few hundred indigenous Tasmanians that were left were then relocated to **Flinders Island**, a small island located north of Tasmania. As they spoke many mutually incomprehensible Tasmanian Aboriginal languages, the Tasmanians were forced to create the so-called **Flinders Island lingua franca**, a mixture of many of these. Unfortunately, the number of Tasmanian languages declined rapidly after the relocation, and it is believed that due to intermarriage and a switch to English, even the Flinders Island lingua franca disappeared at the beginning of the twentieth century.

However, in 2018, the film *The Nightingale* was made, in which some characters speak the Tasmanian language. Was it a true Tasmanian language that was used in this Australian film, full of bloody and violent scenes (just like nineteenth-century Tasmania was), or was a new language invented? The answer to that question is, 'Yes and yes, the **palawa kani** language was used.'

Palawa kani is an artificial language, created by combining available words from all Tasmanian languages, primarily from the east of the island. The language is based on several lists of words from different languages of Tasmanian peoples, as well as a small number of audio recordings of recent speakers. In this way, palawa kani was created, a language that does not just represent one, but all Tasmanian languages, united into one whole. The authorities of lutruwit (Tasmania in palawa kani) approved dual names for some toponyms, in both English and palawa kani. An example of this is Mount Wellington, whose new name in the palawa kani language is *kunanyi*.

Palawa kani is developing nicely, so today it is increasingly possible to hear small children proudly counting in the (almost) language of their ancestors:

1	2	3	4	5
pama	paya	luwa	wulya	mara

6	7	8	9	10
nana	tura	pula	tali	kati

MORIORI

The **Moriori** dialect or language is spoken by the indigenous inhabitants of the **Chatham Islands** (**Rēkohu** in Moriori: 'misty skies'). This archipelago belongs to New Zealand and is located about 800 kilometres east of South Island.

The **Moriori** people are of **Māori** origin. Their ancestors left New Zealand around the year 1500 and settled in the Chatham Islands, where they created a new language, partly understandable to speakers of the **Māori** language. They also developed new traditions, including making carvings on trees, and a lifestyle based on complete pacifism. The basis for this way of life was *Nunuku's Law* (Nunuku-whenua was the head of Moriori from the sixteenth century), which completely forbade war, murder or cannibalism. They spent their lives peacefully, until the middle of the nineteenth century when a group of 900 Māori reached this lonely island, killed a number of their distant cousins from the New Zealand mainland, and enslaved the rest, with a ban on the use of their language.

The Moriori language (**te re Moriori** in Moriori) is a dead language today, but there have been recent efforts towards its rejuvenation: a dictionary and a list of familiar words have been made, and a smartphone app aims to encourage young people to start learning the language of their peaceful ancestors.

Moriori carvings,
usually found on trees

Fig 1.

Fig 2.

Fig 3.

Fig 4.

EAST ASIA

HACHIJŌ

The island of **Hachijō-jima** is located in the Philippine Sea, south of Japan. 1,200 kilometres away lies the small archipelago of **Daitō-jima** (**Daitō Islands**). Despite the great distance between them, a common language connects Hachijō-jima and Daitō-jima, and it is not the standard **Japanese** language.

The **Hachijō** language (known by its speakers as **shima kotoba**, meaning 'island speech') is a very specific dialect of Japanese, or a small separate language within the **Japonic** language family. It is the last remnant of the former **Eastern Old Japanese** language, characterized by a specific vocabulary and numerous archaic features.

Today it is spoken on the islands of Hachijō and nearby **Aoga-shima**, which in the Middle Ages served as a destination for expelled political and other opponents. The significant isolation of these islands has contributed to the preservation of the old language, though today it is still considered to be endangered. Hachijō-jima (63 square kilometres in area) is home to 7,500 people, of whom several hundred – mostly elderly – speak this language; Aoga-shima (9 square kilometres) is home to about 170 people, and almost everyone speaks their old dialect.

Daitō-jima are located about 350 kilometres from the island of **Okinawa-jima**. The archipelago, although known about for hundreds of years, was neither occupied nor inhabited until the very end of the nineteenth century, when it was officially annexed to the **Japanese Empire**. At that time, a group of several dozen speakers of the Hachijō language had settled on the islands in order to cultivate sugar beet; they brought with them the language, which is still spoken by a large number of islanders today.

Characteristic walls on the island of Hachijō-jima

JEJU

Jeju Special Self-Governing Province is the most southerly of South Korea's nine provinces and the only one with autonomous status. It consists of the large island of Jeju (over 1,800 square kilometres and 700,000 inhabitants) and a number of smaller islands. In the centre of Jeju Island, at a height of 1,950 metres, is Mount Halla (or Halla-san), the highest mountain in South Korea.

What makes the island and the province of Jeju different from the rest of Korea is the language spoken by about 5,000 of its residents. The language shares the name with the island on which it is located and is known by its speakers as **Jeju-mal** ('Jeju speech'). In the city of **Osaka** in Japan, there is also a large community of emigrants from the island of Jeju, many of whom speak the language of their ancestors well.

Most Koreans, even those from the southernmost parts of the Korean Peninsula, have great difficulty understanding Jeju. One possible explanation for this is that the island was inhabited by speakers of Japanese or a related Japonic language until the fifteenth century. When Koreans settled in large numbers in the fifteenth and sixteenth centuries, the language of the previous population was suppressed, though not before it had influenced the language of the Korean immigrants, thus creating a new language. Also, during the thirteenth and fourteenth centuries, when the Mongol Yuan dynasty ruled China and the Korean Peninsula, a large number of Mongol soldiers was stationed on Jeju Island, but not in semi-autonomous Korea, which also had a significant impact on the island's language.

The individuality of Jeju Island is also reflected in the sculptures known as *dol hareubang* (*dol* means 'stone' in **Korean**, while the word *hareubang* comes from Jeju language and means 'grandfather'). These sculptures represent deities, and their purpose is to give protection from all kinds of dangers, with a gentle smile from a friendly grandfather. There is a similarity between the dol hareubang from Jeju Island and the moai sculptures from Easter Island (Rapa Nui).

Dol hareubang, Jeju, South Korea

FORMOSAN LANGUAGES

The Austronesian language family is one of the most widespread language families in the world and began its spread from the island of **Taiwan** several thousand years ago. Today, Austronesian languages are spoken in the area bordered by four islands: Taiwan in the north, Madagascar in the west, Easter Island in the east and Chatham Island in the south. This language family is divided into ten branches, nine of which are located on the island of Taiwan alone (550,000 members), while the remaining branch – the **Malayo-Polynesian** languages – covers hundreds of islands in the Indian and Pacific Oceans, as well as parts of the Southeast Asian mainland. It has 385 million speakers, divided into more than 1,200 languages.

The nine branches on the island of Taiwan (25 million inhabitants in total) are usually called **Formosan** languages, after the old Portuguese name for Taiwan (allegedly, the first Portuguese sailor to see Taiwan in the distance shouted, 'Ilha formosa!', which in Portuguese means 'beautiful island'). Formosan languages were once spoken right across the island, but after the settlement of various Chinese ethnic groups, Taiwanese indigenous peoples represent less than 2.5 per cent of today's total population. There are more than twenty-five Formosan languages, of which ten are extinct and another five are threatened with extinction.

Orchid Island (known in Chinese as **Lan Yu**) is located some 65 kilometres southeast of Taiwan. It has an area of 45 square kilometres and just over 5,000 inhabitants, 800 of whom are **Han Chinese**, while the rest belong to the **Tao** Austronesian ethnic group.

Most Tao people on Orchid Island speak the Austronesian language **Tao** (**ciriciring no Tao** in Tao, 'human speech'; **Yami** in Chinese) which, despite its proximity to the island of Taiwan, does not belong to the Formosan languages, but is a Malayo-Polynesian language. Specifically, Tao belongs to the **Batanic** languages, a dialect continuum spoken on an island chain between the Philippines and the island of Taiwan; Orchid Island is the northernmost link in that chain. The Tao settled on this island about 4,000 years ago from the island of Taiwan, which has been confirmed by genetic analyses.

Boats of the Tao people in Formosan Aboriginal Culture Village, an amusement park in Taiwan

SARIKOLI

Iranian languages are usually divided into two major groups: **Western**, the largest of which are Persian (including the **Dari** dialect of Afghanistan and **Tajik** language of Tajikistan) and **Kurdish**; and **Eastern**, whose most important members are **Pashto** (or **Pushtu** or **Afghani**) and **Ossetian**. Most of the Eastern Iranian languages are spoken in Afghanistan and Tajikistan, as well as in small areas of Pakistan and China. **Pamir** languages – a particular group of Eastern Iranian languages – are spoken primarily in and around the Pamir mountain range, most of which lies in Tajikistan. These dozen languages and dialects belong to the group of endangered languages, although they have about 100,000 speakers.

The easternmost of all Iranian languages is **Sarikoli**, spoken by 20,000 people. This is the only Iranian language whose homeland is China or, to be more specific, **Taxkorgan Tajik Autonomous County** in southern Xinjiang (Taxkorgan or Tashkurgan is the capital, formerly known as Sariqöl or Sarikol). This autonomous region is located along the Sino–Tajik border and the great Sarikol mountain range. In China, the Sarikoli language is officially called the Tajik language, although Sarikoli has only distant connections with the eponymous official language of neighbouring Tajikistan. In fact, Sarikoli belongs to the group of Eastern Iranian languages, while Tajik is a Western Iranian language.

Sarikoli does not have an official written form, although the **Uyghur Arabic alphabet** is increasingly used for that purpose, which is not strange, considering that Sarikoli children go to schools where classes are conducted in the **Uyghur** language. For communication with other language groups, Chinese and Uyghur are used. A small number of Sarikoli speakers live in Pakistani-controlled parts of **Kashmir**.

There are archeological finds from a cemetery more than 2,500 years old which suggest that the area of today's Taxkorgan Tajik Autonomous County could have been one of the first areas to follow the ancient religion of Zoroastrianism or even the birthplace of what is possibly the world's oldest continuously practised religion. Probably the oldest evidence of the use of cannabis for religious or ritual purposes was also found in the cemetery.

MANCHU

Manchuria, a historic region in northeastern China, is home to the **Manchu** people. With more than 10 million members, the Manchu represent the largest ethnic community of **Tungusic** peoples and one of the largest national minorities in China. Between the twelfth century and 1912, when monarchy in China was abolished, several Manchu dynasties ruled over China, including the Qing dynasty, the last ruling house of the **Chinese Empire** (1644–1912).

Manchurian rulers and the elite brought their language with them, but they soon began to use the **Chinese** language. This resulted in a rapid decline in the use of the **Manchu** language in the capital Beijing, which was then followed by a more gradual decline in Manchuria itself. After several centuries, we have now reached a time in which fewer than 100 (a hundred!) out of over 10 million Manchurians are fluent in their language. The largest number of Manchu speakers (**manju gisun** in Manchu) today live in **Sanjiazi**, a relatively isolated village in the northeastern Chinese province of Heilongjiang. The village has more than 1,000 inhabitants; 65 per cent are ethnic Manchurians, but only the fifty oldest of them speak Manchu.

At the end of the eighteenth century, a large group of Manchurians, named **Xibe**, was transferred to the Chinese Far West. Many of them have remained in the area to this day, where the **Qapqal Xibe Autonomous County** was formed, and of the 160,000 inhabitants, over 60,000 are ethnic Xibe or Sibe. The language of this ethnic group, also called **Xibe**, is a dialect of the Manchu language. As a language, Xibe has been influenced less by Chinese than Manchu, but it contains some Russian loanwords. The script used to write Xibe is a modified **Manchu script**. Xibe is taught today in some schools and universities of Qapqal Xibe Autonomous County, and there are also some newspapers and several radio and television shows in this dialect. There are frequent visitors from Manchuria and the rest of China, whose aim is to improve their knowledge of the former imperial language by spending time among native speakers.

THAI ENCLAVE IN SINGAPORE

Singapore is a city-state on the island of the same name between Malaysia and Indonesia. It is located in the Straits of Malacca, one of the busiest sea routes in the world. The total area of the Republic of Singapore is slightly less than 730 square kilometres (about the same size as the island of Anglesey), and the population is 5.7 million, 61 per cent of whom are Singaporean citizens. The official languages are English, Malay, **Mandarin** and Tamil, but even in Singapore there is enough space for a few miniature language islands.

The **Golden Mile Complex** is a large residential and commercial building in central Singapore, built in the Brutalist architectural style and completed in 1973. The building, which contains several hundred shops and offices as well as a large number of apartments, is in a state of disrepair, and suggestions have been made to demolish it and for a new development to be built on the 1.3-hectare site.

However, what sets this complex apart is the fact that it represents a kind of **Thai** enclave in Singapore, with a large number of the building's shop owners and residents originating from Thailand. The mall, which occupies the lower floors, has several Thai restaurants, numerous travel agencies organizing trips to Thailand, shops with Thai products, and entertainment venues playing Thai music (among the locals, these clubs are known as *siam diu*, Siam being Thailand's former name). It is therefore not surprising that this mega-building has earned the nickname *Little Thailand*.

WEST ASIA

KHANTY &
MANSI

R U S S I A

KAZAKHSTAN

DUNGAN
(FERGANA VALLEY)

DUNGAN
(CHU VALLEY)

Black Sea

TURKMENISTAN

BRAHUI

C H I N A

I R A N

Mediterranean Sea

BRAHUI

ZOROASTRIAN DARI

PAKISTAN

SAUDI

KUMZARI

ARABIA

OMAN

MEHRI

FAIFI

SHEHRI

Bay of
Bengal

YEMEN

RAZIHI

SOQOTRI

INDIAN OCEAN

KHANTY AND MANSI

Khanty-Mansi Autonomous Okrug-Yugra is an autonomous region within Russia.
It occupies the central part of the West Siberian Plain, and economically represents
one of the most important parts of Russia, since more than 50 per cent of Russian
oil is produced in this area. The Yugra has about 1.5 million inhabitants, and the
two peoples after whom the autonomous region was named (**Khanty** and **Mansi**)
today make up only 2 per cent of the population.

Despite the small numbers of speakers, the Khanty and Mansi are still trying to keep their respective languages from being forgotten. Both languages are very similar and belong to the Uralic languages, a language family of about 25 million speakers, spread primarily across northern Asia and Europe.

The **Khanty** language, formerly known as **Ostyak**, is spoken today by 9,000 people – out of a total of 31,000 Khanty in all of Russia – mostly in Western Siberia. The language has more than fifteen dialects.

The **Mansi** language is the closest relative of Khanty, but has fewer than 1,000 speakers out of 12,000 members of the Mansi people. This language is also divided into several dialects, largely incomprehensible to each other. According to folklore, the ancient Mansi fighters rode moose into battles with their enemies!

Today, Khanty and Mansi write their languages in the adapted Cyrillic alphabet, though there is a linguistically close group of Central European people in which some members use a kind of runic script! According to many (but not all) linguists, Khanty and Mansi are related to Hungarian. Within Hungary there are some that still use the **Old Hungarian script** (**rovásírás** in Hungarian), also known as **Hungarian runes**, although it has nothing to do with Germanic runes. This script actually originates from the **Old Turkic script**, alphabet of the early Turkish states in Central Asia, used between the eighth and tenth centuries.

Sign at the entrance to a Ukrainian city written in Russian (Cyrillic) and Hungarian (Latin and 'rune')

DUNGAN

The **Hui** people are one of the recognized national minorities in China, although they are ethnically and linguistically related to the Han Chinese. The reason for treating the Hui as a separate ethnic group is their belonging to the Islamic faith. Almost all Hui speak only Chinese, with knowledge of certain Arabic and Persian words necessary for performing Islamic religious rituals. In the former Soviet Union and Xinjiang Province in China, Hui are known as **Dungan**, although they call themselves Hui (**Huejzw** in Dungan).

The **Dungan** language (**Hueyzû yüyan** in Dungan) belongs to the group of **Sinitic** (**Chinese**) languages, spoken today by more than 100,000 people in Central Asia, more precisely in **Fergana Valley** and **Chu Valley**. Fergana Valley stretches through northern Tajikistan, eastern Uzbekistan and parts of southern Kyrgyzstan, while Chu Valley occupies northern Kyrgyzstan and southern Kazakhstan. Dungan is based on the **Mandarin** dialects of the Chinese provinces of Gansu and Shaanxi; it is the only Chinese language written in Cyrillic. Formerly, it was written in **Xiao'erjing script**, which is a special type of Perso-Arabic script adapted for Mandarin Chinese. *Huimin bao* (Хуэймин бо in Dungan: 'Hui newspaper') is published in Kyrgyzstan, and is the only newspaper in the world in this variant of Mandarin Chinese.

Due to its isolated position, Dungan has retained a large number of archaisms, and due to its surroundings, it contains borrowings from the Persian, Russian and Turkish languages. Today, there is limited mutual understanding between Dungan and different Chinese languages and dialects.

It is believed that the Dungan people immigrated to their present territory in the second half of the nineteenth century from northwestern China, after an unsuccessful rebellion against the Chinese authorities.

Dungan Mosque in Karakol, Kyrgyzstan

KUMZARI

Musandam Governorate is one of the eleven governorates that make up Oman. It consists of the strategic peninsula of Musandam – which monitors the passage of oil tankers through the Strait of Hormuz between the Arabian Peninsula and Iran – and the small Omani exclave of Madha, which is surrounded by the United Arab Emirates (UAE). (And within this Omani exclave is Nahwa, an even smaller UAE counter-enclave.) The entire Musandam Governorate itself represents an exclave of Oman, since the territory of the UAE separates it from the rest of the home country.

In the far north of the Musandam Peninsula is the village of **Kumzar** (or **Kumza**), where several thousand people speak the **Kumzari** language, the only Iranian and the only non-Semitic language spoken on the Arabian Peninsula. A small number of speakers also live on the nearby Iranian island of **Larak**. Kumzari is very similar to the Persian language, although it contains a large number of loanwords from **Arabic** (which is not surprising, since Arabic is the official language of Oman and all other countries on the Arabian Peninsula). Unfortunately, this language is in danger of imminent extinction, because most young people prefer to learn and use the more advantageous Arabic language. There is no schooling in Kumzari, nor any official literature.

Kumzari people are Muslim, though their traditions also encompass a number of folk beliefs. Almost all the inhabitants of the village of Kumzar reside there only during the colder months; during the unbearably hot summer months, they move to their homes in **Khasab**, the capital of Musandam Governorate, where they inhabit a separate district of the city.

Kumzar village, Oman

SOUTH ARABIAN LANGUAGES

Afroasiatic is a large family of languages, whose 300 tongues are spoken in North Africa and the Middle East. **Semitic** languages are the most widespread group of Afroasiatic languages, spoken by over 330 million first-level speakers. The Semitic language family can be divided into several subgroups: **Eastern** (whose members became extinct a long time ago), **Central** (the most notable languages of this group include Arabic and **Hebrew**) and **Southern** (which are further divided into **Ethiopian Semitic** languages and extinct **Old South Arabian** on the one side and **Modern South Arabian** on the other).

Although the Old South Arabian languages became extinct, there are two languages in use that are considered to be their possible descendants. These languages are:

- The **Razihi** language, which is spoken by 60,000 people in northeastern Yemen, around **Mount Razih (Jabal Rāziḥ)**. In terms of the origin of Razihi, experts are divided into two groups — one believes that it is an Arabic language, which has been greatly influenced by the Old South Arabian languages; the other believes that it is the direct successor of Old South Arabian with loanwords and certain grammatical rules from the Arabic language.

- The **Faifi** (or **Fifi**) language is another possible successor to the Old South Arabian languages, spoken today by 50,000 people around **Mount Faif (Jabal Fayfā')** in southwestern Saudi Arabia, 40 kilometres from Mount Razih.

Both of these languages are considered endangered, because young speakers are rapidly switching to Arabic or moving away from the area in search of better jobs; the prevalence of available media in Arabic also weakens the position of these relatively small languages.

Men with traditional flower hats and a typical settlement at Mount Faif

Modern South Arabian languages, with numerous archaic characteristics of Semitic languages, are spoken in parts of **Yemen** and **Oman** today. Their closest relatives are the Semitic languages of Ethiopia and Eritrea, and the next in line are the Old South Arabian languages. Today there are a few Modern South Arabian languages:

- **Mehri** has about 165,000 speakers in Oman and Yemen.

- **Soqotri** is spoken by 70,000 people in the Yemeni archipelago of **Socotra** between the Arabian Peninsula and the Horn of Africa. The isolation of these islands enabled unhindered development of the language, which now has numerous characteristics that are not present in other Modern South Arabian languages. However, Soqotri is considered an endangered language because the Arabic language, thanks to numerous immigrants from the mainland, is increasingly spreading. The opinion of the state is that Soqotri is only a dialect of Arabic, and not a separate Semitic language.

- **Shehri**, spoken by 25,000 people in the southern part of Oman, near the border with Yemen.

ZOROASTRIAN DARI

Zoroastrian Dari is one of the northwestern Iranian dialects, spoken by about 8,000 to 15,000 **Zoroastrians** in the heart of Iran (the Zoroastrian religion was the main religion of Persia for centuries, until the Islamic conquest of that ancient empire in the seventh century). Most speakers today live in and around the cities of **Yazd** and **Kerman**. Despite its similarity in name, Zoroastrian Dari is not a close 'cousin' of **Dari**, a dialect of Persian and one of the two official languages in Afghanistan (the other is Pashto).

Zoroastrian Dari is also known as the **Behdināni** ('language of the people of good religion') and is divided into two main dialects: **Yazdi** (near the city of Yazd) and **Kermani** (you guessed it: around the city of Kerman). Interestingly, the Yazdi dialect can be further divided into almost thirty separate and mutually difficult-to-understand speeches, each of which is spoken in one Zoroastrian district of Yazd. Both dialects are endangered today, while Kermani is on the verge of complete extinction.

In the city of Yazd, there is a *fire temple* – one of only thirty remaining Zoroastrian temples outside India, where most of the believers and temples of this ancient religion are located. There is also the *Dakhma* ('tower of silence'), a round tower on which 'heavenly burials' used to be conducted by leaving the bodies of the deceased to vultures. The purpose of this was to avoid burying or burning the dead, so as not to pollute the earth, water or air, which are considered sacred in Zoroastrianism. The Dakhma is no longer used for this purpose.

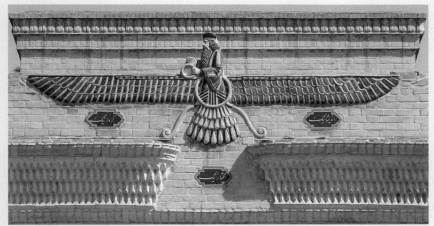

*Faravahar, a symbol of Zoroastrianism and Iranian national identity
(detail from the Fire Temple in Yazd)*

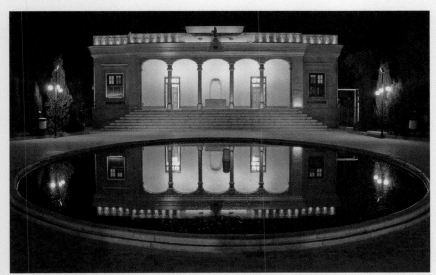

Zoroastrian Fire Temple in Yazd, Iran

BRAHUI

Dravidian languages are one of the basic language families spoken in modern times in southern India and northern Sri Lanka. The total number of speakers exceeds 220 million, and the three most numerous languages from this family are Telugu (84 million), Tamil (75 million) and Kannada (43 million). Although Dravidian languages are concentrated mainly in the south of the Indian subcontinent, speakers of one Dravidian language have chosen an area 1,500 kilometres away – the south of Pakistan – as their home.

Brahui is a Dravidian language spoken by a few hundred thousand people of the same name in the central part of the province of **Balochistan** in Pakistan. It is not clear how the **Brahui** people came to be living in this location, but two theories seem the most plausible: according to one theory, the Brahui are a remnant of Dravidian settlers from present-day Iran, who for some reason did not want to continue on their migration to southern India; the other theory is that the Brahui settled in southern India with other Dravidian peoples, but that at some point they decided to move back, towards a possible ancestral homeland.

As far as is known, Brahui is the only Dravidian language that was never written in a **Brahmic script**, but in a Perso-Arabic script. Recently, a Latin alphabet adapted to this language was created (*Brolikva*, Brahui Roman Likvar). In Quetta, the capital of the province of Balochistan, *Talár*, the only daily and weekly newspaper in the Brahui language, is published.

A small number of Brahui now inhabit **Merve**, also known as the Merve Oasis, which is located near today's city of Mary in southeastern Turkmenistan.

EUROPE

FINNIC LANGUAGES

The area of Northern Europe between the Baltic Sea and the White Sea is largely inhabited by **Baltic Finnic** peoples; **Finns** and **Estonians** make up over 98 per cent of these peoples.

One of the remaining small groups of Finnic peoples are the **Livonians** or **Livs** (**līvlizt** in Livonian), who mainly inhabit the northern parts of **Latvia**. Today, there are fewer than 300 of them worldwide, of which approximately 200 are in Latvia. Throughout history, Livonians have spoken their **Livonian** language (**līvõ kēļ** in Livonian), which is very close to **Finnish** and **Estonian**. It is believed that today there are slightly fewer than fifty speakers at the level of a second language and several hundred who have a basic knowledge.

At the end of the twentieth century, the Latvian government created the **Livonian Coast** (**Līvõd rānda** in Livonian, **Lībiešu krasts** in Latvian), an area of cultural protection for Livonian culture and language. This is an area in the extreme northwest of Latvia, which consists of a coastal area 60 kilometres long, and in which there are twelve Livonian villages. One of these settlements is **Miķeļtornis** (**Pizā** in Livonian; thirty inhabitants), known for having the tallest lighthouse in Latvia.

Votic or **Votian** (**vaďďa tšeeli** in Votic; ten speakers) and **Izhorian** or **Ingrian** (**ižoran keel** in Izhorian; 150 speakers) are another two Finnic languages spoken in the **Ingria** region (roughly, the area between St Petersburg in Russia and Narva, the easternmost city in Estonia).

Lighthouse in Miķeļtornis (Pizā), Latvia

TURKIC LANGUAGES

The origin of the **Turkic** peoples is not clear, although one theory is that some of their ancient ancestors left the area of today's northeastern China 5,000 years ago and reached Eastern Europe via Mongolia and Central Asia. There are approximately thirty-five Turkic languages, the most widely spoken of which are **Turkish** (76 million), **Azerbaijani** (33 million) and **Uzbek** (27 million).

Gagauz is a Turkic language spoken by 150,000 people in Moldova and Ukraine. The political centre of Gagauzia is located in the **Autonomous Territorial Unit of Gagauzia** in Moldova. Their language is part of the **Oghuz** languages, a subgroup of Turkic languages, to which Turkish, Azerbaijani and **Turkmen** also belong. The Russian empress Catherine the Great approved their settlement in the far south of Russia on one condition: that all Gagauz became Eastern Orthodox, which they accepted, so today they represent one of the few Turkic Orthodox peoples.

Unfortunately, the situation with the Gagauz language is by no means good: all official documentation and websites are in Russian, as is schooling.

The country of Turkey is the largest area where Turkish is spoken, but there are also several smaller Turkish-speaking islands. One of these is the town of **Mamushë** (**Mamuşa** in Turkish, **Mamuša** in Serbian), 15 kilometres north of Prizren, Kosovo*. This settlement has about 5,500 inhabitants, of which 93 per cent are Turks.

Somewhat further south, in western North Macedonia, is the municipality of **Centar Župa** (**Merkez Jupa** in Turkish), which is on the border with Albania. This municipality has about 6,500 inhabitants, of which 80 per cent are Turks. Experts from North Macedonia would say that these Turks are actually Macedonian Muslims, also known as **Torbeshi**.

In the same municipality is the village of **Kodžadžik** (**Kocacık** in Turkish) with the family home of Mustafa Kemal Atatürk, the founder and first president of the Republic of Turkey.

*Kosovo is recognized as an independent country by the UK, USA, most European Union member countries and just over half of all UN members. Many other countries do not recognize it, including Serbia, Russia and China.

Crimean Tatar (**qırımtatar tili**) is a language spoken on the **Crimean Peninsula** and in the diaspora, primarily in **Uzbekistan**. It belongs to the group of **Kipchak Turkic** languages (the most well-known of which are **Kazakh**, **Kyrgyz** and **Tatar**). Today, about 260,000 Crimean Tatars live in Crimea, while there are 150,000 in Uzbekistan, a consequence of Stalin's forced deportations during and after the Second World War due to cooperation with the Germans; there are Crimean Tatars in **Romania** (about 25,000) and in **Bulgaria** (3,000).

Crimean Tatars in traditional dress

KALMYK

For centuries, a branch of Mongol peoples known as the **Oirat Mongols** tried to take control of the expanses of Inner and Outer Mongolia, but in the mid-eighteenth century, the Chinese Empire finally won the battle. A consequence of this Chinese victory was the migration of a large number of Oirat Mongols to the west, the furthest destination being the land of the **Kalmyks** (**Hal'mgud** in Kalmyk).

The Kalmyks are a subgroup of the Mongols who, from the mid-seventeenth century, inhabited the western shores of the Caspian Sea, where the **Republic of Kalmykiya**, an integral part of Russia, is still located today. This republic is the only political entity in Europe in which Buddhism is the most practised religion.

The forcible deportation of Kalmyks on Stalin's order also had severe consequences for the **Kalmyk** language (**Hal'mg keln** in Kalmyk), officially known as **Kalmyk Oirat** (**Hal'mg Ôôrdin keln** in Kalmyk); today Kalmykiya has more than 180,000 inhabitants, but only 80,000 speakers of this Oirat dialect – primarily the elderly – which is why UNESCO considers it a 'definitely endangered' language. The Kalmyk language is largely mutually intelligible to those who speak the Oirat dialects in Mongolia and China, although Kalmyk, for understandable reasons, has a large number of loanwords from Russian and Turkic languages.

At the end of the First World War, civil war between the 'Reds' (communists) and the 'Whites' (anti-communists) continued in Russia. After the defeat of the Whites, several hundred Kalmyks, who had fought on their side, fled to the then Kingdom of Yugoslavia. In 1929, they built what was probably the first Buddhist temple in Europe outside of Russia, in the Yugoslavian capital of Belgrade. The Belgrade neighbourhood of Konjarnik (in Serbian, *konj* = horse; *konjarnik* = horse-breeding area) was named after the large herds of horses that the Kalmyks reared in the area. Unfortunately, there are no other traces of the Kalmyk people in Belgrade: the temple was severely damaged during the Second World War, and twenty years later it was completely demolished. Kalmyks from Belgrade fled to the United States, fearing retaliation from the Soviet Red Army, and **Freewood Acres**, New Jersey, is now one of their main centres there.

Chess, a game enjoyed by Kalmyks, in Elista, the capital of Kalmykiya

KHINALUG

Northeast of the Caucasus mountains, west of the Caspian Sea, is the homeland of the **Northeast Caucasian** languages, also known as the **Caspian** languages. These languages are mostly spoken in Russia (in the republics of **Dagestan**, **Chechnya** and **Ingushetia**) and the northern part of **Azerbaijan**; the largest language of this family is **Chechen**, which is the mother tongue for a third of the Caspian language speakers.

Khinalug (**kätš mic'** in Khinalug) is a language that forms a separate branch within the Caspian languages family. About 3,000 people use it for informal communication in the village of **Xınalıq** (**Kətş** in Khinalug) in northeastern Azerbaijan, while official Azerbaijani is used for all official and educational purposes. As the village is located at an altitude of 2,200 metres, it is partially or completely inaccessible for more than half the year due to snow, which aids the preservation of the local language. It is interesting to note that Khinalug has nineteen cases, which is probably the largest number in all European languages, and that, as with some of its neighbouring languages, it has four genders: male, female, animal and inanimate objects.

Panoramic view of Xınalıq village, Azerbaijan

JUHURI

At the eastern end of the Caucasus mountain range is **Qırmızı Qəsəbə** (**Gyrmyzy Gasaba** in Russian: 'Red Town'), probably the only wholly Jewish town outside of Israel and the United States. The town is located in northeastern Azerbaijan and inhabited by about 4,000 **Mountain Jews** or **Caucasus Jews**, also known as **Juhuri**.

It is believed that the Mountain Jews reached the Caucasus – then part of the **Persian Empire** – in the fifth century BC. They have survived to this day by living in the high mountains and hard-to-reach valleys of present-day Azerbaijan and Dagestan, and have fiercely defended their territory, which is how they have come to be known as hardened warriors and horsemen. The main centre of this group of Jews is Qırmızı Qəsəbə, once known as the *Jerusalem of the Caucasus*.

The Mountain Jews of the Caucasus, including 'Red Town', speak **Juhuri** or **Judeo-Tat**, a dialect of the Persian language enriched with numerous expressions and words from Ancient Hebrew.

Juhuri is closer to modern Persian than other Iranian languages from this part of the world (for example, Kurdish). Until the beginning of the twentieth century, the **Hebrew alphabet** was used, which was replaced by Latin after the First World War, and soon after that by Cyrillic. Today, the Hebrew alphabet is being increasingly used.

Six Dome Synagogue, Qırmızı Qəsəbə, Azerbaijan

AFRICA

KORANDJE

The **Songhay** or **Ayneha** is a group of related languages and/or dialects that are mostly spoken in large cities along the Niger river including Timbuktu, Gao – the former capital of the mighty **Songhai Empire** – and Niamey, the capital of Niger. Songhay languages are divided into two groups: **Northern** and the more numerous **Southern**.

Korandje (**kwạra n dzyəy** in Korandje: 'village's language'), one of the northern Songhay languages, is spoken by about 3,000 people out of a total population of 5,000 in the oasis of **Tabelbala**, in western Algeria, 150 kilometres from the border with Morocco. This city is the only place in Algeria where the majority of the inhabitants speaks neither Arabic nor **Berber**. However, although Korandje belongs to the Songhay language family, it has been highly influenced by Arabic and Berber, which are the official languages of Algeria. For instance, the inhabitants of the Tabelbala oasis use Arabic names for all numbers except one (*a-ffu*), two (*inca*) and three (*inẓa*), and only 40 per cent of the words in Korandje are of Songhay origin. The **Tasawaq** language, spoken around the city of **Ingall** (also written as **In-Gall**) in Niger, is believed to be the closest relative of the Korandje language. Unfortunately, Korandje is not taught in schools, and a decreasing number of parents are passing it on to their children, as they believe that it is more useful for them to learn Arabic well.

CLICK LANGUAGES

A small number of languages in Africa (and one invented one in Australia) stand out from all other languages by their use of the so-called *clicks* or *click consonants*. Such are the sounds that express disapproval or pity (in British English *Tut-tut* or *Tsk! Tsk!* in American English) and a similar sound is used in many languages of the Mediterranean area as a substitute for answering 'no' to the question asked. More recently, **Click** languages have gained prominence as a result of the South African film *The Gods Must Be Crazy*, in which the main character Xi, who lives with his Saan (or Bushmen) tribe in the Kalahari, speaks one of the Click languages.

The languages in which clicks are used belong to the now obsolete Khoisan languages family. Today, the prevailing view is that what were regarded as the three branches of the Khoisan language family (**Khoe**, **Tuu** and **Kx'a**), which are predominantly spoken in **Namibia**, **Botswana** and **South Africa**, are actually separate language families, whose common features stem from their geographical proximity. The remaining two languages that were in this family, **Sandawe** and **Hadza**, are usually treated as language isolates.

The language **Taa** or **!Xóõ** belongs to the Tuu family and is known for (probably) the largest number of phonemes; modern research has counted more than 200 consonants and vowels, while English speakers have fewer than 45 separate sounds at their disposal. This language is distinguished by the large use of consonants, and also by the fact that more than 80 per cent of words begin with a click, as represented by the '!' at the start of a word, along with other symbols.

In Taa, the word *Taa* means 'human', while the full name of the language (**tâa ǂâã**) means 'people's language'. As for counting, Taa expressions are used only for the numbers one (ǂʔûã), two (ǂnûm) and three (ǁâe), while the other numbers are borrowed from neighbouring languages. The total number of speakers is about 2,500, most of whom live in the border area of **Botswana** and **Namibia**.

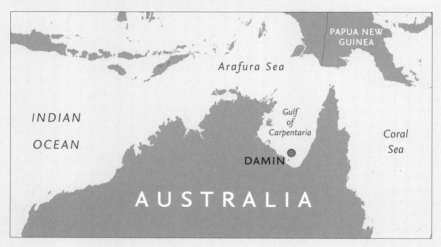

On the other side of the Indian Ocean, in **Australia**, is the **Damin** language, the only language outside Africa that contains clicks. Damin is a ceremonial language, used by dedicated members of the First Nation peoples of **Lardil** (**Kunhanaamendaa**) and **Yangkaal** in the Gulf of Carpentaria, northern Australia. Unfortunately, the languages of Lardil and Yangkaal are now almost extinct, and with this many traditions are fading, so Damin language is not conversed in today. The gradual revival of the traditions of these peoples provides some hope that Australian clicks may soon be heard again.

SIWI

Jlan n isiwan is the local name for the **Siwi** language, the easternmost Berber language and the only Egyptian indigenous Berber language spoken in the **Siwa** and **Qara** oases. These two oases, located in Egypt not far from the Libyan border, are now inhabited by more than 30,000 people, who use Siwi in their daily communication. However, the Egyptian authorities do not recognize the existence of this language, so it is not used in schools or in the media.

In ancient times, the Siwa Oasis was known as the site of the oracle of Amun, which is why Siwa was called the *Oasis of Amun Ra*. It is known that Alexander the Great visited this sanctuary after his army conquered Egypt. During the **Ptolemaic Kingdom** – the Hellenistic Egyptian monarchy, whose last ruler was the famous Cleopatra – the oasis was known as the *Field of Trees*.

Remains of the temple of the Egyptian deity Amun Ra and the mosque in the Siwa Oasis; the Field of Trees is visible in the background

NORTH AMERICA

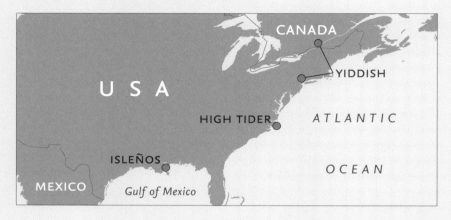

HIGH TIDER

Isolated communities around the world often develop a new dialect or language from their existing one.

This is exactly what happened on **Outer Banks**, a string of barrier islands and spits that separate the large lagoon of Pamlico Sound from the Atlantic Ocean in North Carolina. This area is known as the home of the **High Tider** or **Hoi Toider**, one of the specific dialects of the American English language. An alternative name for this dialect is **Ocracoke Brogue**; Ocracoke is a town on the island of the same name, part of Outer Banks, and *brogue* describes a pronounced accent (especially Irish or Scottish) when speaking English. Centuries of isolation have indeed led to a different development of the local dialect, which can sound a bit like the Irish or Australian accents. However, modern times have led to an increasing number of tourists in this area, as well as an increasing use of electronic media in standard American English, which is why fewer than 200 people speak this old dialect now, and there is little chance that that number will grow.

A term often used as the name of this dialect, Hoi Toider, comes from a rhyme by which locals often explain to outsiders – *dingbatters* in Ocracoke Brogue – the difference between their speech and standard English: *Hoi toide on the saind soide* ('It's high tide on the sound side', where 'sound' is Pamlico Sound).

ISLEÑOS OF LOUISIANA

Isleños are residents of Louisiana, United States, who originated from the Canary Islands, a Spanish autonomous community located on the archipelago of the same name 100 kilometres off the coast of Morocco. The ancestors of the Isleños ('islanders'), about 2,000 of them, settled around the Mississippi Delta during the short-lived Spanish colonial rule in the late eighteenth century. They later mingled with other ethnic groups in the area, such as the French, Creoles, immigrants from the Philippines and Latin America, and others. Over time, there were more and more descendants, but the relative inaccessibility of the American South (swamps, watercourses, dense forests) has helped this Spanish dialect endure even to this day. The remaining speakers, mostly in their 80s, are now concentrated in **Delacroix Island** and several surrounding fishing villages. Delacroix Island is not really an island, but a part of the mainland surrounded by endless swamps and wide streams of slow plain rivers.

Los Isleños Fiesta is a large festival held every year in St Bernard Parish, the city with the largest number of Islanders' descendants, and which celebrates Canarian heritage, music and food.

Dancing at Los Isleños Fiesta

YIDDISH LANGUAGE ISLANDS

The most referenced Jewish languages in our time are Hebrew and **Yiddish**, and the main differences between them are:

- Hebrew is a Semitic language, just like Arabic and **Ethiopian Amharic**, and is spoken by 10 million people, primarily in Israel.

- Yiddish is essentially a dialect of German, with a large number of words from Slavic and some from the Romance languages. It is spoken by 2 or 3 million members of the Jewish diaspora, mostly in the United States, the UK, Canada and Sweden.

Until recently, **Kiryas Joel** was a village within the city of Monroe, in New York State. The village was formed in the early 1970s by **Hasidic Jews** (an Orthodox Jewish community), but problems arose when its area expanded with its growing population. After numerous quarrels and conflicts, a referendum decided to make the village of Kiryas Joel part of the newly formed city of Palm Tree. Today, Kiryas Joel has almost 30,000 inhabitants, who use Yiddish in all spheres of communication (only 6 per cent of the inhabitants use English at home, 92 per cent use Yiddish and 2 per cent Hebrew). Most women leave work after the birth of their second child in order to dedicate themselves completely to raising children; families in Kiryas Joel are large, usually with six to ten children, which explains the need to extend the boundaries of this community. The inhabitants of this city live according to strict religious and social rules, and the basic code of conduct is displayed at the entrance to the city, so that it may be followed out of respect for the locals.

Kiryas Joel is not the only Yiddish-speaking language island in North America. **Monsey** is a resort within the city of Ramapo, Rockland County, New York State. Today, almost 25,000 people live in Monsey, of whom 41.5 per cent speak Yiddish and 7 per cent Hebrew. Interestingly, completely encircled by Monsey is the village of **Kaser**, whose 5,000 inhabitants are Hasidic Jews. The village was founded in 1990 and is today the most densely populated municipality in the State of New York – the population density is higher even than that of New York City. In the city of Ramapo there is another wholly Hasidic Jewish village: **New Square**. Its 8,500 inhabitants belong to the Square Hasidic Movement, which originates from the city of Skvyra, Ukraine.

Further north, in the town of Boisbriand, southwestern Quebec, Canada, is **Kiryas Tosh** (or **Tash**), a Hasidic Jewish community with about 3,000 inhabitants. It was named after the village of Tash (now Nyírtass), located in northeastern Hungary, not far from the borders with Ukraine and Slovakia.

Although Yiddish is written in the Hebrew alphabet, it is also possible to use the Latin alphabet for this language. Here is a comparison of the same passage from *The Little Prince*:

Yiddish (in Latin alphabet):
Oy! Kleyner prints, bislekhvayz ho ikh farshtanen dayn kleyn melankholish lebn. Gor lang, iz dayn eyntsike farvaylung geven di ziskeyt fun di zunfargangen. Ot dem nayem prat hob ikh zikh dervust dem fertn tog in der fri ven du host gezogt: Ikh hob zeyer lib di zunfargangen.

Hebrew (in Latin alphabet):
Hoy, nasikh katan! Kakhah hevanti, me'at me'at, et khayekha haze'irim hanugim. Yamim rabim lo hayta lekha ela hana'ah akhat viykhidah: no'am shki'ot hashemesh. Haprat hekhadash hazeh noda li bayom harevi'i baboker, keshe'amarta: Ani ohev et shki'ot hashemesh.

Aerial view of Kiryas Joel in 2014

SOUTH AMERICA

KARIPÚNA FRENCH CREOLE

The first half of the nineteenth century led to a revolution in the far north of Brazil, caused by the poverty of a large part of the population as well as frustration among the local elite over its lack of influence in the state policy of the **Empire of Brazil**. This led to numerous migrations from the Amazon Delta to the Oyapock or Oiapoque river, which today represents the border between French Guiana and Brazil. Among these migrants was the tribe of **Karipúna**, which maintained a close connection with the peoples and tribes of French Guiana. The consequence of this close contact was that members of the Karipúna people completely stopped using their language at the beginning of the twentieth century; instead, they began using custom French Guianese Creole, known today as **Karipúna French Creole** or **Lanc-Patuá**.

Most of the vocabulary of this language is of French origin, except for the part concerning the rich flora and fauna of the Brazilian state of Amapá, located between the Oyapock river and the Amazon Delta. This tribe is the easternmost extent of the **Kalina** or **Caribs** people, who inhabit the region of northern South America covered by Venezuela, Guyana, Suriname and French Guiana.

The people of Karipúna number 2,000 to 3,000, spread across more than ten villages. The largest of these is **Manga** with more than 1,000 inhabitants. Today, all variants of the Karipúna French Creole language are endangered, as the younger and middle generations have largely switched to Portuguese.

Celebration of Dia do Índio ('Indian Day') in Manga, Brazil

PIRAHÃ

Pirahã people are one of the indigenous peoples of Brazil, numbering about 800 members. They live in the Amazon rainforest along the **Maici** river, a tributary of the Madeira river. They call themselves **Hi'aiti'ihi**, roughly translated as 'the straight ones'.

The **Pirahã** language is used by fewer than 400 people, but it is not considered endangered, because speakers use it on all occasions, while the use of the Portuguese language is spoken minimally and in a very limited form.

In many ways, Pirahã is one of the simplest languages. For example, it is believed that there are only eight consonants and three vowels, though this does not prevent communication by whistling, which Pirahã men often use while hunting.

The language only has the numbers one and two, though they equate more to the terms 'little' and 'much'. This makes even simple addition an unknown concept to the Pirahã people. It seems that there are no names for colours at all, only terms that mean 'light' and 'dark' (which could perhaps identify with the words 'white' and 'black'), while descriptive expressions are used for other colours, for instance red is 'like blood'. Although their language is relatively simple, Pirahãs are true experts on living and surviving in the jungle. Daniel Everett, linguistic anthropologist, once said about Pirahã people: 'They can walk into the jungle naked, with no tools or weapons, and walk out three days later with baskets of fruit, nuts, and small game'.

There are few languages in the world that use whistling as a form of communication. One is **Silbo Gomero** ('Gomeran whistle'), which is used on **La Gomera**, Canary Islands, Spain. There are also whistling speeches in the village of **Kuşköy** in northeastern Turkey, the village of **Aas** in France, not far from the border with Spain, as well as **Sfyria**, a 2,500-year-old whistling speech of the village of **Antia** on the island of Evia (Euboea), Greece. The unusual practice of giving children 'singing names' (*jingrwai lawbei*) in the isolated Indian village of **Kongthong** is reminiscent of these whistling speeches, with one difference: in Kongthong everyone gets a name that sounds like a bird song, but this singing is only used when calling someone by name, not for full communication.

PALENQUERO

Palenquero or **Palenque** (**Lengua** in Palenquero: 'language') is probably the only **Spanish Creole** language in South America spoken in northern Colombia. Palenquero originated as a mixture of the **Kikongo** (**Kongo**) language, which is spoken today around the Congo River in Africa, and Spanish. Although the **Palenqueros** ethnic group numbers nearly 7,000 people, fewer than 3,000 know this Creole language; others, especially the young, speak Spanish more often today.

Today, most Palenquero speakers live in the village of **San Basilio de Palenque**. The village was founded in the early seventeenth century by runaway enslaved people, together with a small group of indigenous Americans; the leader of this successful rebellion was Benkos Biohó, an enslaved man from one of the royal families of an archipelago in modern-day Guinea-Bissau. As there were people of different ethnic and linguistic origins among those who escaped, it was necessary to adopt a common language. This was based on the Kikongo language, the mother tongue of most of the group, with many Spanish expressions added in. Language, tradition and music have been retained, as a symbol of defiance against the former enslavers.

Palenquero women are known for their colourful dresses and street fruit sales

GLOSSARY

Amish – members of a Protestant sect who separated from the Mennonites in the seventeenth century. They live a traditional rural life

Australian Kriol – a language that originated as a mixture of English and various indigenous languages around Sydney; it later spread throughout Australia and then became extinct everywhere except in North Australia, where it became the mother tongue of more than 30,000 people

Brahmic script – a member of a family of writing systems used throughout the Indian subcontinent, Southeast Asia and parts of East Asia

Byzantine Empire – also known as the Eastern Roman Empire, the continuation of the Roman Empire in south-eastern Europe and Asia Minor, which ended in 1453

Carinthian dialects – a group of closely related Austro-Bavarian dialects of the German language spoken in Carinthia (today divided between Slovenia and Austria)

condominium – (from the Latin *con-dominium*: 'joint ownership') means the joint management and authority of two or more states over a particular territory

creole – a language that has developed from a mixture of two different languages, one of which is generally European. It incorporates features of each and has become the mother tongue of a particular community

Cyrillic alphabet – a script used for the writing of some Slavonic languages, primarily Russian, Bulgarian and Serbian. It was derived from the Greek alphabet

diaspora – a dispersion of people originally belonging to one nation or speaking a common language

enclave – a territory completely surrounded by the territory of another state. More is written on enclaves in the author's other book, *The Atlas of Unusual Borders*

ethnically homogeneous – describing an area or place where all the inhabitants are of the same cultural or racial origin

exclave – part of a territory or state that can only be reached from its home territory by passing through another territory or state

Gallo-Italic languages – a group of Romance languages of Northern Italy, also spoken in San Marino, Monaco, and parts of Switzerland and southeast France

Holy Roman Empire – the complex of western European territories under the rule of the Frankish or German king who bore the title of Roman emperor, between the years 800 and 1806